# Cellular Obsession

How Smartphones, and the Internet of Things Are Going to Change Your Life

Copyright © 2016 / 2017 Nick Vulich

Nick Vulich All Rights Reserved
ISBN: 1546616314
**Cover Illustration**
© Can Stock Photo Inc. / bbbar
http://www.canstockphoto.com

# Table of Contents

Getting Started .................................................................................. 6

Mobile Will Change Everything – Again ....................................... 13

    Data ............................................................................................... 16

    APPs ............................................................................................... 21

    Price .............................................................................................. 30

    Device Innovations ...................................................................... 36

    Augmented Reality, Pokémon Go! How It Got a Hundred Million Downloads ...................................................................... 46

    Virtual Reality – Opening a New Window on the World ........ 51

    Contextual Intelligence .............................................................. 57

    Beacons ........................................................................................ 66

    Security ......................................................................................... 76

    Mobilegeddon ............................................................................. 86

    5G - the Future of Cellular ......................................................... 90

    What's Next ............................................................................... 103

The Internet of Things .................................................................. 110

    Drones ........................................................................................ 113

    Wearables .................................................................................. 120

- Medical Innovations ............................................................. 133
- Connected House ................................................................ 139
- Connected Car .................................................................... 153
  - Infotainment Systems ..................................................... 159
  - Connected Car Simulators ............................................... 166
  - Autonomous and Semiautonomous Driving ..................... 169
  - Ford Pass ....................................................................... 177
- Meet the Experts ................................................................... 180
- About the Author .................................................................. 183
- Bonus Excerpt ....................................................................... 185

# Getting Started

**W**hether you're ready for it or not, the future is here, and it's going to change everything. If you think the Industrial Revolution changed the way Nineteenth Century Londoners lived, you haven't seen anything yet.

Your future is going to be a blend of Jules Verne, Arthur C. Clarke, Isaac Asimov, and a thousand Fifties and Sixties B-movies combined. Robots are going to be a part of your future, as are super-fast spaceships, stealth weapons, and crazy ass politicians. But, most of the changes that happen are going to be more subtle. You probably won't notice them until they become ingrained in your day-to-day routine. Think smartphones, texting, Facebook Messenger, and dozens of other apps you use every day. It seems like they've always been there, right?

That's the way most social changes happen. They occur gradually over time.

Social changes occur when someone, or group of someones, gets a bug up their butt and begin advocating for change. That's what happened in the 1950s and 1960s. The changes they wrought were slow and hard fought. Most of them, we take for granted today.

During the 1960s and 1970s, the Hippies protested the Vietnam war. They advocated for an end to the war, and for the legalization of marijuana. Fifty years later, most Americans would agree the Vietnam War was a mistake, and should never have occurred. Individual states, such as Colorado and Oregon, are currently rewriting substance abuse laws, and legalizing marijuana for medical and recreational uses.

For centuries, the pace of change has been painfully slow, inching along at a snail's pace. But, the Internet has changed all of that. Changes that used to take decades, or centuries, now take place in as little as six months.

Change today begins in an inventor's garage, with an idea gnawing at the back of some creative's head, or with a computer programmer trying to solve an issue important to a small group of people. Someone shares their discovery with a friend, who shares it with another friend. The next thing you know—the project goes viral on Twitter, Facebook, and Instagram. Suddenly, everyone and their brother is hopping on the bandwagon.

In the past, most changes happened so slowly you couldn't tell they were happening.

Alexander Graham Bell invented the telephone in 1876. The few people who were in the know considered it a play toy, rather than a useful invention. It was cool, but no one saw a practical use for it. The spread of the telephone was painfully slow during its first few years. In 1877 Bell had 3,000 subscribers. By 1878 that number had climbed to 10,000 phones in service. In 1900 there were telephones in over 600,000 homes and businesses. Still, success was anything but certain.

The next generation saw unparalleled growth. By 1923 Bell Telephone[1] reported there were 14,050,565 telephones in the United States. Phone installations skyrocketed after World War II. Then just as quickly, cell phones killed the landline. Ten years ago, nine out of ten households had landlines. Today (according to a Center of Disease Control and Prevention[2] report) that number has dwindled to approximately two in ten households.

The first mobile phones debuted in St. Louis, Missouri, on June 17, 1946. The network could only handle a maximum of twenty calls for the entire metropolitan area.[3] The first portable phone you could carry around with you hit the market in 1983. It weighed two pounds, had a thirty-minute talk time before it

---

[1] *Telephone Tribute*. Web. http://www.telephonetribute.com/timeline.html
[2] Blumberg, Stephen J. and Luke, Julian. *Wireless Substitution: Early Release of Estimates from the National Health Interview Survey, January – June 2014*. National Health Interview Survey Early Release Program. 2014.
[3] *Milestones in AT&T History*. Web. http://www.corp.att.com/history/milestones.html

needed to be recharged, and sported a hefty price tag of $3995. Fast forward to 1996; cell phones were still waiting for their breakthrough moment. Prices remained high, and most people continued to look at mobile phones as futuristic devices. Over the next few years, prices fell, and ownership skyrocketed. Here we are in 2016. Over 90 percent of adults in America own a cell phone, while landlines are well on their way to extinction.

A similar evolution was playing out with computers.

I graduated from high school in 1976, the same year two California inventors, Steve Wozniak and Steven Jobs, were banging around in their garage, pounding out the first Apple computer. By the time I graduated from college in 1980, personal computers had just started to go mainstream. Users had their choice of *Tandy*, *Timex-Sinclair*, and *Commodore*, among other brands. The IBM PC didn't exist yet. IBM didn't announce the PC until August 12, 1981.

The U S Census Bureau[4] reported just 8.4 percent of U S households owned home computers in 1984. By the year 2000, 51 percent of Americans owned a home computer, and 41 percent had home internet service. Today, 84 percent of Americans own a PC or tablet, and 73 percent of households have access to broadband internet. That's a 74 percent increase in

---

[4] *Computer and Internet Use in the United States: 2003*. U. S. Census Bureau. October, 2005.

computer ownership in just over thirty years. What's even more remarkable is broadband Internet use soared from zero to 73 percent in a twenty-year period.

In 1980, IBM approached Bill Gates, a Harvard Business School dropout, to develop an operating system for their new personal computer (PC). Gates purchased licensing rights to a program called *86-DOS* from *Seattle Computer Products* and modified it for use with the newly released IBM PC. In return, he received a one-time payment of $50,000 from *IBM*. *Microsoft* released the first version of its Windows operating system in 1985.

APPs were virtually unknown in 2007. A decade later we can't get along without them.

During that short thirty-year period from 1985 to 2015, *Microsoft* rocketed from a virtually unknown company to the most well-known software company in the world. *IBM* is still the big kid on the block when it comes to computer hardware, but their mistaken belief that hardware was where the money was at, not software—cost them hundreds of billions of dollars in profit.

Another Harvard dropout, Mark Zuckerberg, created a website that changed the way over a billion people communicate. *Facebook's* first release, known as *Facemash*, was shut down by Harvard University just days after its first appearance. The Harvard-only site was extremely popular among students, but it quickly sucked up the school's bandwidth, knocking out several of their servers. Students complained about privacy violations because Zuckerberg posted student pictures and profiles without their permission.

Since its inception on February 4th, 2004, *Facebook* has changed the way users communicate and share personal and professional information. In twelve short years, it has gone from a Harvard-only thing to a worldwide phenomenon that helps over 1.2 billion users keep in touch. Currently, 200 million people use the *Facebook Messenger* APP to text back and forth, rather than use device based texting. That number is only going to grow as more people download the APP.

Another 500 million people use *WhatsApp*, an APP that lets users text back and forth without incurring SMS charges. In the long run, *Facebook Messenger*, *WhatsApp*, and similar offerings are going to totally change the way we communicate. They're also going to knock the cellular industry for a loop, as smartphone users continue their current shift away from talking to text only communication.

*Facebook* has also revolutionized the way we share information. Every time you post a picture, video, or comment, you allow 1.2 billion potential *Facebook* users to discover what's going on in your private life (depending on your privacy settings). Five years ago, it would have taken a professional investigator a full week to discover the amount of personal information they can learn about you from a five-minute visit to your *Facebook Timeline*.

When you think about it, that's scary.

A computer program has coaxed us into willingly sharing our most private moments, ones we've been taught to safeguard carefully. And, the even scarier thing is—you haven't seen anything yet.

GPS location services already let everyone know where you are and where you have been. Close-up photos from *Google Maps* can pinpoint you going into and out of your home, school, place of work—everywhere.

If we aren't careful, personal privacy will soon become a thing of the past.

**Why all this talk about computers**, software, and inventors in a book about the cell phone? Because they're all converging into a device so small, it fits in our pockets, but so powerful, you could run a large business or small country from it.

It's crazy, but it's true—until they implant a cellular chip in our heads, the cell phone is going to continue to change the way we live, think, and communicate.

If you're ready for a glimpse into the future, read on.

# Mobile Will Change Everything – Again

O ur love affair with our cell phones will grow even stronger over the coming years.

A recent study conducted by PEW University[5] says over 44 percent of us have slept with our cell phones. Are you listening Victoria's Secret? This behavior could signal an opportunity to market mobile nighties and other assorted cell phone lingerie.

Honestly, cell phones are changing the way we live, work, shop, receive news and other information. Most Americans under age eighteen don't know what a landline is and have never lived in a home that had one.

---

[5] *Mobile Technology Fact Sheet.* Pew Research Center, Internet, Science, & Tech. 2016.

Here are some other facts you need to wrap your head around if you ever hope to understand these changes.

1. 78 percent of teens own a cell phone, 47 percent of those teens who own cell phones, own a smartphone. (PEW University study[6])
2. 90 percent of adults own cell phones, 64 percent of American adults carry smartphones.
3. 34 percent of teenage girls age 14-17 access the internet only through mobile, compared to 24 percent of boys the same age. (PEW University study[7])
4. Social media is killing desktop computers. 47 percent of Facebook users accessed the site only through mobile in 2015, up from 34 percent in 2014. (eMarketer[8])
5. Google recently updated their search metrics to favor mobile. Since the inception of its 2015 *Mobilegeddon Update*, websites not optimized for mobile are being removed from or moved to the bottom of search results. (WSJ Digits[9].
6. The Apple Watch is changing the way users pay. During the short time it's been available, 80 percent of users are choosing to make payments with it—instore, and

---

[6] *Mobile Technology Fact Sheet*. Pew Research Center, Internet, Science, & Tech. 2016.
[7] *Teens and Technology* 2013. Pew Research Center. March 13, 2013.
[8] *Trends for 2016: Six Predictions for What Will Happen*. eMarketer. December 14, 2015.
[9] *Google's 'Mobilegeddon' Was a Big Deal, After All*. WSJ Digits. July 15, 2015.

online. Android device owners have similar options with their devices.

What does it all mean?

Mobile devices such as cell phones, tablets, and wearables will play an expanded role in our everyday life.

More, and more, of us, are going to be romancing our cell phones, dragging them in and out of bed with us every night.

Right now, most of us consult our cell phones for advice before we make an important decision. A J D Powers[10] survey shows 96 percent of car buyers shop the Internet before they visit the dealership. Finance managers are watching deals meltdown as savvy shoppers hop online to search for better deals while they wait for the finance office to complete paperwork. That's good news for consumers, bad news for car dealers.

**Okay, change is going to happen.** Everybody gets that. The real question is what kind of changes we should expect?

Here's a little peek into what industry experts see coming down the pipeline.

---

[10] *New-Vehicle Buyers Who Spend the Most Time Shopping Online Also Visit the Most Dealerships.* J. D. Powers. McGraw Hill Financial. September 9, 2014.

# DATA

**C**ell **phones, tablets, and mobile devices** will continue to replace laptops and PCs. *Time Magazine*[11] recently reported 63 percent of smartphone users jumped onto their devices to access the internet. And, it's that shift towards mobile data that's helped to enrich cellular carriers. A PEW University study says cellular companies generate more revenue from data charges than from voice fees.

George Gracin III says, "...the shift towards mobile computing is greatly favoring smartphones. A few years ago, tablets were predicted to overtake phones as the larger used platform for mobile computing and silence the PC/Laptop. We were definitely wrong about that, but we didn't really foresee phones overtaking computers for most of the personal internet usage."

It's all part of a trend created by the introduction of the first smartphones. We are shifting to a culture of the internet on the

---

[11] Luckerson, Victor. *Landline Phones Are Getting Closer to Extinction*. Time Magazine. Web. July 8, 2014.

go. Users want to be able to access the internet wherever they go—on the beach, at work, in planes, cars, and automobiles.

Cellular companies are responding by dishing up larger data packages at ever faster speeds. Within the next five years, all carriers will offer inexpensive unlimited high-speed data. T-Mobile has offered an unlimited data plan for some time now. AT&T jumped on the unlimited data bandwagon in mid-January of 2016. Verizon joined the party in early 2017. It's a major step forward for users accustomed to paying hundreds of dollars for monthly data overage charges. Unlimited data plans offer high use cellular junkies a certain peace of mind. They can go crazy, without going broke.

City governments could be the biggest threat to cellular companies and local internet providers. Municipalities are running feasibility studies to discover what it's going to take to create the *wired city*. They're looking at laying fiber optic networks throughout the city and taking over the internet business. And, it's not just about money. Cities and States have uncovered a have, and have not, gap in access to broadband internet. Prices have spiraled out of control. A good portion of the population, especially in low-income areas, can't afford broadband service. For students, and minority business owners, that places them at a significant disadvantage.

One city exploring such a plan is Davenport, Iowa. The city has already laid over 100 miles of cable and invested $600,000 in building a fiber optic network to connect the city's computers. The city is currently conducting feasibility studies to determine what's next. They want to go into the internet business but need to be sure the investment in infrastructure will pay off over the long haul.

Another Iowa City, Cedar Falls, operates one of the oldest city-owned Internet services in the country. An article in *Yes Magazine*[12] says users there have faster internet speeds than most nearby Iowa cities and pay an average of $200 per year for their service. When you compare that to the $400 to $1000 per year charged by other broadband carriers in Iowa, the savings to subscribers is significant. Internet speeds are also significantly faster. Cedar Falls Utility (CFU) launched super-fast Gigabit service in 2013, making it the first city in Iowa to offer Gigabit service.

And, that's not to slight established broadband and cellular carriers. Many of them have partnered with retailers, malls, and other businesses to provide wifi hotspots everywhere.

---

[12] Alperovitz, Gar and Hanna, Thomas M. *These Cities Built Cheap, Fast Community-Owned Broadband. Here's What Net Neutrality Means for Them.* Yes Magazine. February 23, 2015.

**Helsinki, Finland, was one of the first cities** in the world to offer "completely" free public wifi. Back in 2006 when Helsinki began exploring internet coverage for their government office buildings, they decided to offer free wifi for city residents as well. The service has been a win for residents and travelers to the city. Users can access free wifi on the go, from just about anywhere in the city.

KETV 7[13] in Omaha, says Council Bluffs, Iowa, is in the process of deploying "free" wifi throughout the city. But, city officials caution, it's not something designed to replace your home wifi. The city broadcasts low band wifi to power resident's personal devices while they're on the go.

New York City pioneered an initiative, nicknamed LinkNYC, where they converted over 9,000 obsolete phone booths into wifi hotspots. The unique thing about the project is private companies are funding it, not the government. *Governing Magazine*[14] reports, each of the refitted phone booths will contain a computer screen, telephone, and port to charge your device. Users can make free calls, and access information from the built-in terminal. Other users, within 150 feet of the phone booth can tap into gigabit internet service.

---

[13] *Council Bluffs closer to city-wide Wi-Fi*. KETV 7/Omaha. June 10, 2015.
[14] Marshall, Alex. *NYC's Plan for Free Citywide* Wi-Fi. Government Magazine. February, 2015.

The bad news is, we're still going to need cellular carriers and home internet providers into the foreseeable future. The good news is, service is going to be faster, and less expensive. Cable company monopolies will gradually disappear as municipalities continue to wire towns and broadcast free low-band wifi for people on the go.

# APPs

Smartphones wouldn't be what they are today without APPs. A 2015 report published by ComScore[15] says APP engagement accounts for 54 percent of the time mobile users spend on the internet. The truth is, APP usage is up 90 percent in the last two years. *Facebook, Facebook Messenger,* and *What's App* are a good part of the reason for that, as is *Angry Birds, Candy Crush*, and similar games.

It seems as if we can't get enough APPs. Millennials especially, can't wait to get their hands on the latest creations. Millennials are the people who should be targeted by APP developers if they want to gain traction fast.

Here's another fact that shouldn't come as a surprise to any smartphone user—three-quarters of us pick and choose which APPs we want on our home page. And, there's a good reason for that. Over half the time we spend using APPs occurs on a single

---

[15] *The 2015 U. S. Mobile App Report.* comScore. September 22, 2015.

"favorite" APP. *ComScore* discovered APP position on a user's home screen is an indicator of how popular they are. Apparently, the faster you can get your thumbs on an APP, the more popular it is.

If you're an APP developer, listen up!

Smartphone users don't like to download APPs, especially retailer APPs like Walmart, Target, and Best Buy. They will do it if it is required to get the deal, but once customers have gotten what they want, your APP is going to hit the recycle bin. Lifestyle APPs are a different story. *ComScore* reports APPs that fuel our daily habits, such as Starbucks and Dunkin Donuts, continue to grow in popularity. Consumers are happy to interact with brands that create a great experience and give them a warm fuzzy feeling. Make it faster for users to get what they want, need, and desire, and you'll make the home screen. Make it about yourself, or your company, and you can kiss your APP goodbye.

So be sure to tuck that info away. The easiest way to score prime real estate on a mobile user's home screen is through their stomach. If I were a local restaurant, beverage company, or candy maker, I'd be all over that.

**Over the past several years**, website developers have scrambled to enhance their websites for mobile, but they can only do so much. There's only so much information you can fit onto a small screen and still make it readable. Findability is another problem. As more and more websites compete in search, individual websites become harder to discover. The good thing about an APP is once users have it downloaded to their device, competition becomes a thing of the past. APP providers have total control over the user experience and the information they receive.

Most of the experts I've talked with believe APPs will still be a part of the cellular landscape five years from now. They envision APPs evolving to the point where our devices will be powered by "invisible APPs" that run unseen in the background of your phone's operating system. You can see some of this today in Google Now. But, the experts agree, it's going to be several years before we see this transition become fully implemented. In the meantime, APPs are expected to stay the course. That means you can continue to download more APPs over the short run.

The tricky part is getting people to download APPs in the first place. For savvy shoppers and merchants, it often comes down to a tradeoff. Users surrender space on their devices in exchange for the promise of discount coupons, or other free offers. The key for companies, and for shoppers, is that downloading, and using an APP, needs to be a win-win proposition.

John B. Dinsmore, Assistant Professor of Marketing at Wright State University says, "APPs will be of continuing, and growing importance, but they may change in appearance and function.

The emergence of so-called 'invisible APPs'—Applications which are buried in the phone operating system, or that can be activated by texting certain codes—will continue, as it is increasingly difficult to get consumers to download APPs."

One reason APPs will go incognito is "people are increasingly conscious of the additional sacrifice of privacy of an APP versus accessing a service through a mobile browser." Dinsmore says, "*Facebook Messenger* is a good example. While Messenger is a very popular APP, a large segment of FB users has avoided downloading the APP because of controversy over the APP's use of people's data."

As with anything else, it's a tradeoff. Every time users download an APP or any other program off the internet, they ask themselves, "What's it going to cost me?" or, "Is there a better way to do this?" Dinsmore suggests, "For most people, an APP does not become essential because it's 'a good APP.' It becomes essential because the core service is essential and the APP represents more efficient access (vs. browser access) to that service."

"The thinking is that APPs will continue to be more integrated with one another over the next few years," says Lauren Fellure, a Partner at Snap Mobile. "Users won't go into an individual APP to accomplish a task, rather they will message, or ask for what they need, and APPs running in the background of their devices will take care of their needs. For example, a user might type into a search bar on her phone's home screen, 'I need to find a Mexican restaurant near me,' The phone will open *Google Maps, Around Me, Yelp*, etc. in the background, and serve the best options it finds from all relevant APPs to the user on her home view."

John Dinsmore agrees with this. He says, "People tend to favor a small number of APPs. It's really hard to break into a person's APP library." Space is precious on a smartphone, and face it—who wants all that clutter on their device. One result of that "likely means the rich [will] get richer in mobile—Google, Facebook, and Amazon—because they have the power to port other company APPs through their operating systems or APPs."

A recent article in *Intercom*[16] takes things a step further. They say what's important is the notifications we receive from websites and APPs, not the platforms themselves. One example of this is *Facebook*. Every time someone comments on or likes one of your posts, *Facebook* sends out a notification. The thought is, the notification tells you everything you need to know. Why do you need to visit the website, or check the APP?

What the folks at *Intercom* are suggesting is APPs may still exist as a "publishing tool," or as a "holder" for content, but the

---

[16] Adams, Paul. *The End of Apps as We Know Them*. Web. https://blog.intercom.io/the-end-of-apps-as-we-know-them/

notifications sent by the APP are how most users will interact with it. There's no reason to open the APP itself.

To make this a reality, every notification sent out would need to include a call to action—share, post on *Facebook*, comment, order, etc. And, many of them already do.

**For now, APPs are going to** become more integrated. When you check your bank account, it's going to show you the local weather forecast, news highlights, and stock market results. Store APPs are going to focus more on providing a total customer experience. They will serve up news, entertainment, and shopping trends. That health APP you use to monitor your workout will become more multifunctional. It's going to track your stats, record medical information, display health news, and show users local news and weather reports.

Here's a small taste of what's in store for your bank APP in the not too distant future.

*As you're jogging through Vander Veer Park, it hits you; you forgot to make your car payment. You whisper into your smartwatch, "I need to make my car payment." The built-in voice recognition software pulls up your bank account, shows you the amount due for your car payment, and prompts you to check your account balance before you make your car payment. You fold the screen out so you can see everything better. You notice your* medical reimbursement payment got deposited this morning, and there's a pending transfer from your brokerage account. The money will hit your checking account tomorrow. There's also a message from your personal banker, reminding you about your account review scheduled for Friday.

A quick glimpse at the stock ticker shows your 401K is up 3.25 percent on the day, and just over 21 percent for the year. If your stocks keep growing at this pace, you just might reach that goal of retiring before you hit forty-five. There's another school shooting in the news, and President Trump is telling Americans the wall should be finished by the end of the year. A quick look at sports highlights shows the Cubs are playing the Indians at 4:30. There's no time to waste. You move straight to the restaurant section and place a delivery order.

The delivery boy pulls up just as you reach your condo. You wave your watch over the barcode on the receipt to make your payment. Inside your house, you curl up on the couch and whisper "Cubs / Indians game" into your smartwatch. Your bookcases slide apart, revealing your 96" curved screen TV. Sandwich in one hand, soda in the other, you're ready for the game to begin.

Self-interest is one reason for this change in APP development. The longer you spend on a given APP, the more likely you are to do business with them. Another reason is carrier data caps and excessive data overage charges. Financial concerns are forcing smartphone users to rethink when, and how, they use their devices. One outcome is many users have been forced to limit the number of APPs they use, and download, to their devices. If companies want consumers to continue to use APPs, they need to tailor them, so they better fit user needs. One way to do that is to make their APPs more multifunctional. The more tasks an APP can perform, the more likely consumers are to use it and stay on it longer.

Lauren Fellure thinks APPs of the future are going to be more task focused. Her thought is the APPs that survive "will largely be used to run real-world appliances, and devices that are connected to the internet (i.e. the Internet of Things), such as refrigerators, crock pots, heaters, home security systems, etc."

**What it all comes down to**, is in the short run we're going to see a flurry of new APPs hit the market. Over the long haul, most APPs are going to go "undercover." Instead of pulling up your favorite APP to order lunch, you're going to Google, "Where's a good place for ribs?" Google is going to search a myriad of APPs it has open in the background, and pull up a list of nearby rib joints. Along with the names and addresses of the best places to eat ribs, it will provide a link to reviews, maps, menus, and transportation services.

For new or unknown businesses, this will be a game changer. It's going to level the playing field even more and give new businesses an amazing opportunity to get discovered and find a new clientele. For existing businesses, the competition is going to heat up because it's no longer about your name—That's only one small portion of what search engines look for. It's all about your reputation.

Think of the new generation of APPs as *Google Local on steroids*.

Business size isn't going to mean squat anymore. The businesses that win are going to be the ones that have a ton of social media likes, great reviews, and do the best job of connecting with their customers. That's going to bring them to the front of the new search. The more background APPs they appear in, the more likely it is they will get displayed towards the top of the search.

# Price

**P**erhaps the most noticeable change to the cellular landscape is how the big three carriers are forcing a paradigm shift in the way we purchase our cell phones. For the last twenty years, consumers have been trained to expect a new cell phone upgrade every two years. Our service providers conditioned us to believe we were entitled to a new phone as a reward for being loyal customers and renewing our contract. Today cellular companies have turned the table on us, and are asking us to pay full price for our devices. The new pitch is with no contracts; there are no limits. We are free to upgrade whenever we please.

Here's the lowdown. Two year contracts are dead. T-Mobile killed them off nearly two years ago; Verizon kissed them goodbye in 2015, and AT&T said adios to contracts in early January of 2016.

The newest offer is an installment plan. Just pay the sales tax down, and most carriers will finance the balance over twelve to thirty months. In return, there are no contracts. You can upgrade as often as you like (provided you pay off your old device first).

There is a multitude of reasons for the move away from two-year contracts, but ultimately it's about the money. The new iPhone 7S retails for anywhere between $649 and $969, depending upon the model you choose and how much memory it has. The Samsung Galaxy 8 carries a similar price tag—roughly $750.

That's a lot of money—more than most cellular customers can afford to plunk down at one time and more than most carriers care to give away. Carriers have done their best to keep the entry level price point for a new smartphone affordable by requiring no down payment, and minimal monthly payments.

Industry expert, George Gracin III, explains the change by saying, "The days of only paying $1 in exchange for an iPhone with a 2-year contract are almost gone so the larger smartphone companies like Samsung and Apple may have to rethink strategies. People may not be so keen on paying nearly $800 for a phone, even if it's broken down over 24 months, or much longer."

Even Apple jumped on the installment plan bandwagon in 2015, when they introduced their new *iPhone Upgrade Program*.

Prices start at $32.45 per month, and buyers get an unlocked device they can use with any carrier—no contracts—no commitments. Another advantage is Apple includes *Apple Care +* (a $129 value) for FREE.

National Retailers like Target, Walmart, SAMs, and Costco are feeling the pinch. Now that they can no longer offer a 99-cent or a 99-dollar iPhone, they're finding it harder to lure in new customers. Many stores have begun to offer gift cards with the purchase of a new phone. Last year at Christmastime just about every major retailer offered either a $150 or $250 promo card. AT&T heated things up even more when they offered a BOGO on select Apple and Samsung Phones during the final weeks of 2015. T-Mobile created a similar promotion in January and February of 2016. They offered their most popular devices at half price. Smart consumers who take the time to watch and wait should be able to score some great bargains on their favorite devices.

Expect to see a steady stream of new promotions as cellular carriers and retailers do whatever it takes to fuel sales growth.

**Keep your eyes peeled for lower priced phones** and devices. The major carriers have already turned tablets into a commodity passing them out willy-nilly to anyone with a spare penny, or 99 cents. Providers are making their money on the back end—

charging activation fees, monthly service charges, and mobile data fees.

Over the next several years we're going to see dozens of new smartphones hit the market—many of them from virtually unknown companies. Some of them will be cheap knockoffs, but others will be feature-packed devices, loaded down with the latest gizmos and gadgets users could only hope to find on more expensive models.

George Gracin III says, "Huawei is about to release the *Honor 5X* in North America this year, a metal-encased Android phone with specs that eerily rival the popular *Samsung Galaxy S6,* but an insane price of $199. A startup company called *OnePlus* unleashed what they call the *Flagship Killer*, the *OnePlus 2*, at nearly half the cost of a *Galaxy S6*, but with more memory, more RAM, and Dual SIM capabilities. They're also producing a more modest, yet very affordable alternative, the *OnePlus X*. Motorola (now rebranded as *Moto* by Lenovo) has become quite infamous for making high-spec phones at low prices, with their under-$200, Moto G line, and upscale customizable Moto X line."

Apple recently released the iPhone SE, similar in size to the iPhone 5S. It's priced at a modest $399 and contains many of the same components found in the iPhone 6S. For cost-conscious consumers who want the real thing, the iPhone SE is a great value.

Another phone scheduled to hit the market soon is the *Saygus V Squared*. It has all the bells and whistles you would expect from an ultra-high-end phone, at about the price of a standard iPhone 7S. What's intriguing about the Saygus is it's the first major cellular device financed through a crowdfunding campaign. Their *Indiegogo*[17] fundraiser in 2015, raised a whopping $1,333,986.

The phone itself features up to 464 GB of storage, wireless HD beaming, a 21 Megapixel camera, dual SIMs, and a Harmon Kardon sound system. The Indiegogo site shows 473 phones sold at prices ranging from $600 to $650.

A less expensive option for Android users is the Nexus 5X. It has a 5.2 inch HD display, 2 GB of RAM, 16 or 32 GB of storage, a 12 Megapixel rear-facing camera, and a 5 Megapixel front-facing camera. And, it sells for $379, half the price of a standard Samsung Galaxy S7.

Another inexpensive option is the ASUS ZenFone 2. It's an Android-based device, with a 5.5-inch display, 16 GB of memory, and a 13-Megapixel rear-facing camera. And, here's the kicker; the phone carries a price tag of $199. That's the same price many of us are accustomed to plunking down for a two-year contract replacement. Is it a perfect phone? No, but it does pack a lot of

---

[17] *Saygus V Squared*. Web. https://www.indiegogo.com/projects/saygus-v-squared#/

extras for the money. The only drawback I can see is its plastic case.

**It's obvious there's a huge market** out there that will gobble up full featured devices for $199 or $299. It's just a matter of who's going to cash in and woo them away from Apple, Samsung, and LG. If they are smart, the big three device makers will introduce "lite" models of their smartphones, and crush the competition before it gains a foothold. It may mean less profit up front, but over the long haul it would protect their market share and help to weed out upstart device makers.

Time will tell how they react.

For now, it appears as if ATT, Verizon, and T-Mobile are out to grab as much of the business as they can. One promotion offered customers a free iPhone 7 if they traded in their old iPhone 6, 6S, 6Plus, or 6S Plus. For many consumers, it was a deal too good to pass up.

Looking beyond the trade-in offer, it means the price of refurbished and like new iPhones should take a tumble. Whether the companies choose to offer them on their websites or farm them out on eBay and Amazon through resellers, it means a lot of pre-owned iPhones are going to hit the market just in time for Christmas.

# Device Innovations

**D**evices themselves are changing, both internally and externally.

Screens are getting bigger and changing shapes. The Apple iPhone 6 Plus, 6S Plus, and 7 Plus; and the Samsung Galaxy Note 4 and Note 5 (and the flaming Note 7) all have larger displays. The LG Curve and Samsung Galaxy 7 Edge are experimenting with curved screens to provide a better viewing experience. Roll up, and fold up screens, are in the pipeline as another method to expand screen size.

Camera quality continues to improve. The iPhone 7S has a 12-megapixel rear-facing camera and a powerful 5-megapixel front-facing camera. The Samsung Galaxy 7 sports a 16-megapixel rear-facing camera, and a 5-megapixel front-facing camera. The newest generation of phones can record 4K HD video. The iPhone 6S has a feature called *Live Photo* that lets you replay the precious moments before and after you took the picture, and the *Pro Mode* on the Samsung Galaxy 6 gives you precision control and focus when capturing images.

Manufacturers are investigating new materials that will make smartphones and their screens almost indestructible. Just about every manufacturer is tackling battery technology, trying to unravel the secret of how to extend battery life. One promising innovation is a self-charging battery now being put through its paces by Nokia.

**It's no secret battery technology** trails other developments in cellular innovation.

Apple claims the new iPhone 7 has a capacity of fourteen hours talk time (on 3G networks), and twelve hours for internet usage (on 3G, 4G, or LTE networks). That's almost double the battery life of the original iPhone released in 2007, but it's nowhere near enough power for today's cellular junkies. Check out any home, office, or car, and the first thing you're going to notice is a boat load of devices connected to USB chargers.

It used to be people were terrified they would be stranded alone on the highway. Now our worst nightmare is our smartphone battery won't make it through the day.

Manufacturers are experimenting with all manners of technology to relieve this pain, but so far no real solution has emerged.

Apple developed a terraced cell battery for the MacBook that provides up to thirty-five percent more power. What they did was create a series of electrode sheets they can stack into any sized cells they choose. The result is they can fit battery strength to the space available. Apple also redesigned the chemical formula inside the battery for an added power boost. Right now, Apple only uses the technology in the MacBook. In time, it could make its way to Apple's phones and tablets.

David Carroll, a research scientist at Wake Forest Nanotech Center, created a substance called Power Felt. It's fabric that absorbs heat produced from being carried in your pants pocket. Designers say the fabric could boost smartphone battery power by as much as fifteen percent. The thought is if Power Felt is used to line your cell phone case, it can serve a dual purpose, both protecting your phone and extending your battery life.

Another innovation being pursued by Nokia involves the use of graphene. Graphene is the thinnest and strongest material ever created by man. It's more conductive than copper and as flexible as rubber, so it has the potential to transform several areas of cell phone technology.

Nokia[18] says their experimental graphene battery is self-charging. The battery is "capable of regenerating itself immediately after discharge through continuous chemical

---

[18] Borini, Stefano. *Graphene technology for future mobile devices.* Nokia Research Center.

reactions." It can also use humid air to recharge itself, and "exhibits a fast recovery of its voltage within a few minutes after being fully discharged" without applying any external power source.

The way we charge our devices is also changing. Samsung and Nokia recently released a charging pad—just lay your phone down on it, and it begins to charge. There's no more need to search for a power cord or waste a half hour trying to connect it to your phone. Charging pads are easier to use, and because they don't have to plug in their device, consumers are less likely to damage the delicate charging pins inside of their phones.

**Business Korea**[19] defines smartphone screen technology in four distinct stages: curved, bent, foldable, and rollable.

Why should you even care about flexible displays?

1. Most flexible displays are manufactured from OLEDs, which are light-emitting-diodes made from a lightweight plastic material. They provide brighter, crisper displays on an electronic screen while using less power.
2. Because OLED's made from plastic, not glass, there is less chance your display will shatter if dropped.

---

[19] Jin-Young, Cho. *LG Display Completes Development of Transparent Display Technology.* Business Korea. March 24, 2015.

3. The plastic material means your phone will weigh less and can be made thinner than traditional smartphones.

We are currently in stage one of screen technology. LG and Samsung have curved screen devices—the LG G Flex II, and the Samsung Galaxy 7 Edge. Rumor has it Samsung will release a foldable screen smartphone sometime in 2017 that will open up just like a book. Over the next several years, developers are talking about fold up and rollable screens. The day may not be too far off when you can fold your phone up and jam it in your pocket, or maybe it will roll up, and you can wear it like a bracelet or wristband.

The possibilities are endless. But, for now, flexible screen innovations are limited because of device constrictions. Batteries are one of the biggest barriers to flexible screen technology. Batteries are rigid and will remain that way into the foreseeable future. Case technology is another problem. Many companies are experimenting with graphene, a super thin and flexible substance that may soon change the shape and dynamics of current smartphones.

**One of the biggest problems** users experience with smartphones is they're fragile, and they break easily. We take them everywhere we go—to the beach, hiking, work, you name a place, and someone's got a smartphone in their hand, their pocket, or slipped into their bra.

I've seen smartphones run over by cars, crushed in car doors, and run over by a semi on the highway. Those were all total losses. What's more common, is a cracked or scratched screen.

Most smartphone screens are made from glass. It's easy to work with, can be strengthened by adding chemical additives, and can be molded with anti-reflective materials to prevent glare. But, the main thing glass has going for it, is it's cheap. Glass costs just pennies per square inch to manufacture.

When Apple began development of the iPhone 6, they made a big bet on sapphire as a replacement for glass screens. At first glance, sapphire appears to be the perfect material to replace our fragile glass screens. Sapphire is the second hardest material known to man, outside of diamonds. It's extremely resistant to scratches, and supposedly—tougher than dirt. Apple already used sapphire in some of their iPhones as camera lens covers, and to cover their fingerprint sensors, so it made sense to explore extending the technology to screens.

The story has it; Apple dumped nearly a billion dollars into the project to bankroll their partner, GT Advanced Technologies. A *Wall Street Journal*[20] article reported things went sour almost

---

[20] Wakabayashi, Daisuke. *Inside Apple's Broken Sapphire Factory: How $1 Billion Bet on iPhone Screens Failed, "the Boule Graveyard."* The Wall Street Journal. November 19, 2014.

from day one. Eventually, they scrapped the project. GT Advanced Technologies filed for bankruptcy, and Apple ended up manufacturing their new iPhone screens using the same old glass technology.

Tim Bajarin published an article in *Time Tech*[21] that talked about many of the issues involved in using sapphire as a replacement for glass on smartphone screens. Two of the key drawbacks were costs and durability. Glass costs just pennies per square inch to produce, sapphire runs several dollars per square inch. Using sapphire for screens would have raised the price of each iPhone by as much as $100—more than most buyers would have been willing to fork over. The other problem was durability. Even though Sapphire is the second strongest substance in the world, it turns out; it's a poor choice for smartphone screens. Sapphire does an excellent job of resisting scratches, but it's brittle, and it breaks easily when dropped.

So, for now, into the foreseeable future, smartphone screens will continue to be made from glass.

**Manufacturers are always on the lookout** for more durable materials that could make smartphones almost indestructible. SquareTrade (an electronics warranty provider) reports one in three new smartphones wind up in the recycle bin their first year.

---

[21] Barjarin, Tim. *Here's Why Glass Is Still Beating Sapphire.* Time Tech. July 13, 2015.

What makes that number even scarier is all the money consumers plunk down to protect their devices with—OtterBoxes, LifeProof cases, and Gorilla®Glass screen protectors. One of the latest metals considered for use in constructing smartphone shells is graphene, a relatively new material, first developed in 2004. Studies show graphene is two hundred times stronger than steel and extremely resistant to water. It's also very thin, and flexible like rubber.

These are all things that would appear to make graphene the new wonder material for smartphones, but it's still too early to tell. As I mentioned earlier, Nokia is already developing self-charging graphene batteries. Samsung is exploring graphene cases and screens. The American Chemical Society believes touchscreens can be created from a thin layer of graphene, rather than glass. That would enable manufacturers to develop super thin phones that would fold up like paper to fit in your pocket.

Another material researchers are testing for cell phone cases is liquid metal. Liquidmetal was first developed in 2003 and contains a series of amorphous metal alloys consisting of titanium, nickel, copper, and zirconium. The result is a material stronger than the aluminum used in the iPhone. An added advantage is it will not bend. The first full liquid metal phone was released in the United States last year by Turing Robotic Industries. It has several unique characteristics. The liquid metal used in the Turing phone is waterproof, and they coated the circuit board so if water does seep in, it will bounce off, and won't damage the device.

**Cell phones killed the landline phone,** and now smartphones have killed the digital camera. Who needs a bulky camera, and all its assorted gear, when they've got a full featured camera, and a 4K HD video recorder in their pocket?

The new breed of smartphones showcases the latest camera innovations. The Google Nexus 6P has a dual-tone flash system, which *NetworkWorld reported,*[22] "illuminates the shot, enhances colors, and improves contrast in low light." The result is photo resolution that rivals most digital cameras.

No matter how you approach it, smartphone cameras will never be on an even par with digital cameras. Here's why. With cameras, the larger the size of the image sensor, the better the resulting picture. The problem is smartphone cameras have tiny sensors. To get around this, especially in low-lighting situations, manufacturers engineered something called backside illumination (BSL). What BSL does, is move a portion of the wiring behind the sensor, essentially giving the sensor a larger area to perform its task.

---

[22] Patterson, Steven Max. *Google's Nexus 6P boasts the future of Android smartphone cameras.* NetworkWorld. October 26, 2015.

Right now, Apple is poised to revolutionize camera technology in smartphones. They recently acquired a company called LinX. One of LinX's specialties is multi-aperture cameras for cell phones. By having many smaller sensors, they enable the camera to use a smaller lens. Compared with single-aperture devices, multi-aperture devices enable smartphone cameras to take better quality photos.

It's possible the next generation of iPhones will no longer have protruding camera lenses because of this technology. It could also result in a thinner device, because by using multiple sensors, Apple would be able to shrink the thickness of the case required to house the camera. LinX is working on is depth mapping. In its simplest terms, depth mapping would allow people to make 3D scans of objects from pictures taken at different angles.

Smartphone cameras will never rival the quality of photos taken by a full-size digital camera, but for most of us, it doesn't matter. The beauty of a smartphone camera is you always have it with you. You can point, and snap a picture, or shoot a video, and share it almost instantaneously by email, text, or across all your social media platforms.

Most smartphone users aren't looking for the "perfect picture," they just want to capture the moment and share it with their network.

# Augmented Reality, Pokémon Go! How It Got a Hundred Million Downloads

**A****ugmented Reality (AR) will grow** in popularity.

Augmented reality works with all screens and connected devices. It's somewhat like opening the window to a new world. Just point your device, and your smartphone overlays a virtual image onto your screen.

"AR [augmented reality] is PRIMARILY used on smartphones these days, iPads too. But when we develop AR solutions, we're primarily engaging on phone factors," says Chris Nunes, of *The Heavy Projects.com*.

"When explaining [augmented reality] to a new user, I typically use Yelp as a model. Most people have used Yelp these days, and know what restaurant reviews are. Yelp USED to have a feature on their mobile APP that allowed you to hold up your phone in camera mode and see the reviews of all the stores around you, but instead of in a list, the reviews were superimposed on the actual individual storefronts."

Augmented reality provides quick, easy to understand information.

To get started with augmented reality you need to download an APP to your smartphone. The APP uses your smartphone's camera to view your surroundings, and the GPS system on your smartphone to determine your coordinates. Once everything is in place, it takes an existing picture from your camera and blends new info with it, such as images or animations.

To test augmented reality out I downloaded the Augment APP [23] and selected scan to load pictures from the inside of my home into my phone. After that, I selected an image I wanted to overlay on my living room. One minute I watched a giant troll dance across my couch. The next moment an incredibly ugly alien sauntered across my living room.

The beauty of augmented reality is how easy it is to use. You just point your smartphone at something, and it overlays an image on your screen. Tourists can point their phone at a street in front of them, and their phone will show them directions to a restaurant, or art gallery. Companies can embed images in their advertisements. When viewers point their smartphone at it, they see a 3D life-size render of the product.

---

[23] *Augment*. Web. http://www.augment.com/

Augmented reality can also be used to display navigational directions on a car's windshield. Stores can use the technology to let customers try clothes on virtually, or to see how furniture would look in their home before they purchase it. Gamers can use augmented reality to bring characters to life. Trainers can employ it instead of hands on experience.

Lenovo and Google are bringing a whole new version of augmented reality to smartphones near you in 2016. The devices employ Google's Project Tango technology. Google says, "Project Tango combines 3D motion tracking with depth sensing to give your mobile device the ability to know where it is, and how it moves through space."

Essentially Tango will allow your device to map indoor spaces—and locate where the walls, floors, and ceilings are. And, here's the kicker, your device can also pinpoint precisely where it is. You can mark a spot, so someone else can easily find it. Retailers and malls can create maps that direct you to a specific store or location within the store; towns can set up directories that help you find your way around. Gamers can blend mixed-reality and virtual reality using the Google Cardboard VR Headset.

**Pokémon Go! is the most successful** Augmented Reality APP to date. It was downloaded over 100 million times in the first month after its release.

"The app itself took 20 years of preparation," says Keith Fernandez. "Many of those working on the app expected it to have success—just not at the record-breaking rate it did.

"What about the app made it a success?

"When Pokémon first came out on the Gameboy, it took the market by storm," said the twenty-seven-year-old Fernandez, who has fond memories of playing the game as a kid. "It was the first game of its kind to step outside normal level based gaming. It opened up an entirely new world, where the user was free to wander about, and play, however, he, or she, saw fit.

"Pokémon Go! had the same effect with its new augmented reality features. It allowed users to play the game with their phones—combining the physical and digital world for the first time.

"For us 20 to 50-year old's, it re-sparked our love for the game, and, as many would admit, 'it allowed us to relive our teens,' which in today's day and age of chaos, was a refreshing getaway."

**Pokémon Go! Merged the cartoon world** with the real world. It introduced hundreds of millions of people to a new technology and encouraged people to get up out of their recliners and go out into the real world. And, it did it all for free, using a device just about all of us own.

That's the magic of Pokémon Go!

Niantic created the APP, but it was made possible because of Google's Digital Mapping Services.

The game itself seems simple enough.

You wander through the park and discover a Ghastly—lurking behind the outhouse. Across the street, under an apple tree—you spot a Pikachu.

It's not hi-tech—but, there is a certain thrill to it.

As far as the design process goes—you'd think the designers would just throw Pokémon out there. But, the way the founder of Niantic put's it—that's not so.

John Hanke says they decided to make the game more realistic. Rather than just toss Pokémon about all willy-nilly—they placed Pokémon close to their natural habitats. Water Pokémon like Magikarp and Squirtle show up near water. Rock Pokémon like Geodude, Graveler, and Ryhorn are more likely to show up in mountainous areas.[24]

That way the game is more like the story. It ties everything together.

Of course, like anything else—there are problems.

To keep the game safe, designers decided to keep Pokémon away from streets and highways. When people started to complain about damage to cemeteries, designers took Pokémon out of the graveyard.

**The problem with Pokémon Go!** is, "it was not made to incentivize long-term play," says Keith Fernandez. "After level twenty, the game slows down incredibly."

Still, Pokémon Go! Introduced hundreds of millions of new users to augmented reality. It primed the pump—and got developers and users thinking—about what comes next.

New Pokémon is in the mix—that's for sure. Hard-core Pokémon fans are sure to want to catch them all. As technology expands—virtual reality is another possible way to extend the game.

---

[24] Bogle, Ariel. "How the Gurus behind Google Earth created Pokemon G0." Mashable. July 10, 2016.

# Virtual Reality – Opening a New Window on the World

Here's the quick explanation of Virtual Reality versus Augmented Reality.

Virtual Reality (VR) immerses users in the digital world. Augmented Reality (AR) overlays digital 3D objects onto the real word. Or, if you prefer—VR places users inside an entirely computer generated world. AR makes it possible for digital information to appear to be part of the real world.

VR devices (goggles) give users a new way to interact with software programs or APPs. Scott Adam Gordon says VR will change input devices much like the touchpad replaced the mouse on laptops.[25]

Samantha Rivers, writing in *Awesome Techie*, said almost the same thing. Her thought was Virtual Reality headsets are a game

---

[25] Gordon, Scott Adam. "Why virtual Reality Headsets Could One Day Outsell Smartphones." Android Pit. April 25, 2016.

changer. They can take a dinky four-inch screen, and turn it into a screen that "appears nearly limitless."[26]

"The thing that makes VR magical," says Maria Korolov, "is when you move your head, you can look around the virtual world. It tricks your brain into thinking you are there. You don't get the same effect when you play a 360-degree video on a regular phone or tablet.

"Sure, you can turn around, and use it as a window into the world of the video. But you still see the rest of the normal world around you. In a VR headset, your normal world goes away. All you have is the virtual world. You are right there."

"We've already surpassed the idea of the screen," says Wren Handman, with Hammer & Tusk. "Sure, I can put on a pair of goggles and experience a screen that feels as surrounding as IMAX—but why would I do that when I can put on goggles and experience a movie without a screen?" She points to movies like *Invasion*, and *Notes on the Blind* that are already available in VR.

**I look at smartphones as** a gateway drug to Virtual Reality. Everyone has one.

---

[26] Rivers, Samantha. "Why Smartphones are the Future of Virtual Reality." Awesome Techie. July 11, 2016.

Google Cardboard and all those VR headsets Samsung is giving away are convincing people to give it a try. The barriers to entry are so low; no one has an excuse not to give it a whack.

Many people talk about goggles and other gear replacing smartphones. The biggest problem right now is the goggles. They're bulky. They're uncomfortable. People don't like to wear them. Engineers are working to get them down to the size of a regular pair of glasses. When that happens—VR is going to explode.

"Manufacturers are working like crazy to get VR headsets down to the size of sunglasses," explains Maria Korolov, "interacting wirelessly with our smartphones, with built-in cameras to pick up hand gestures, and the ability to change the transparency level so that we can go from VR to MR to AR seamlessly. All the pieces are there. They're being prototyped in the labs, and will be hitting the market in the next couple of years."

For now—it's a waiting game. Technological developments will open a new world in VR, AR, and MR.

At first glance, gaming seems to be the focus of Visual Reality. "That's a myth," says Maria Korolov. "That's where the U.S. media attention is. 360-videos and virtual travel apps are minor events, and big-ticket video games are big ones. There are thousands—tens of thousands—of videos and VR apps—and only a handful of good VR video games, so it's easier to focus on the games. And the big brands are with the games, like PlayStation.

"VR games are the flash and sizzle tip of the iceberg. Videos, travel, education—those are less sexy, but in my opinion, much more important, long-term."

Games are "definitely where the hullabaloo is, but the most exciting applications are definitely outside of entertainment, and they're already beginning," says Wren Handman. "One study is using VR to help paraplegics regain muscle control; putting them into an experience where they see themselves walking can actually help them do it in the real world! They haven't managed to make anyone walk again just yet, but they HAVE regained bladder control, which is a huge quality of life improvement. Other medical uses include treating paranoia, depressing, and phobias, and training surgeons."

It's another case of appearance versus reality. Games are just a small portion of the market for VR applications.

**What was it Avenue Q said?** "The internet is really, really great— for porn."[27] As it turns out, so is VR.

"Porn is huge," says Maria Korolov. "In 360-videos, it feels like you're right there in the room. PornHub already has a dedicated

---

[27]https://www.youtube.com/watch?annotation_id=annotation_87171&feature=iv&src_vid=QKNnwLL991c&v=LTJvdGcb7Fs

VR channel, and a whole bunch of studios are getting into the act." It's giving them an opportunity to "charge for their videos again, so they're investing HUGELY in the technology.[28]

"Meanwhile, everyone on the planet either already owns a smartphone or is saving to buy one. Food? Who needs it! A smartphone is everything, especially in an emerging country."

**So, what's ahead for us.**

"It isn't really well-defined," says Maria Korolov. "Some people use MR to cover everything that's AR and VR. Some people use MR to mean something in the middle (though I'm not sure what that is). Like I said above, I think we'll soon have glasses that can seamlessly take us from one to the other and anywhere in between.

"For example, you could be in a virtual castle, but you can see your friends around you in 'real life.' Or you can sit at your desk, and your desk is real, but the rest of the office around you is a virtual office that you share with colleagues from around the world. Or you could be in your living room, looking at a blank wall, and with a gesture, it will turn into a movie screen. Or you can change the color of the wallpaper around you, or make the walls

---

[28] Even though it's not really relevant—I decided to fact the statement that "the internet was really, really made for porn." As it turns out, less than four percent of internet searches involve porn. Like gaming, and VR—it's a matter of perception versus reality. Ruvolo, Julie. "How Much of the Internet is Actually for Porn." Forbes. September 7, 2011.

disappear completely and put you in the middle of a tropical beach."

At this point, so much is uncertain.

Virtual reality, like 5G, is an evolving technology. Its future is still unwritten.

# Contextual Intelligence

Not too long ago the *MIT Technology Review*[29] published an article that suggested your smartphone wasn't all that smart. As proof, they offered an example of a friend sending you an email about a great restaurant they ate at the day before. The argument was, if your phone is so smart, why doesn't it pull up the collateral information you need to follow up on your friend's suggestion. The way it works now, if you want to know more about the restaurant, you would need to pull up their website to check out the menu, *Google Maps* to get directions, and *Yelp* or another review site to see what other people are thinking. And, if you need a ride to get there, you need to look up Uber, or some other car service.

---

[29] Metz, Rachel. *Artificial Intelligence That Makes Your Phone Smarter.* MIT Technology Review. July 6, 2015.

If your phone can't do that, just how smart is it?

And, that takes us to the core of the current research into contextual intelligence and smartphones. The goal is when you query your phone it should make smart suggestions about what you should do next.

Think about it?

Who knows you better than your phone? The built-in GPS location services know where you go, how often you go there, how long you stay. When you get in your car in the morning to go to work, it knows which route you're going to take. It can anticipate a five-minute stop at the "Kwik Shop" so you can grab a large Diet Coke and cinnamon roll. It knows the parking garage you're going to pull into, and how long your car is going to be parked there.

The same thing goes for when you take the kids to school in the morning. Your smartphone knows what time you're going to leave home, and what time you're going to drop the kids off. It knows what school you're going to, and what time school lets out. It even knows that Wednesday is an early out day.

Now here's the real question. If your phone is so smart, why doesn't it check the weather every morning before you leave? And, if the weather is bad, why doesn't it check for school closings? And, if it was really on the ball, it could shut off your alarm if it determines school is canceled. That way, you could sleep in, undisturbed, and when you do finally get up, you would see the school closing notification on your lock screen.

Let's take it a step further.

Suppose you're getting ready to go on vacation, and a portion of your route takes you from Omaha, Nebraska to Chicago, Illinois. Before leaving home, you Google driving directions using Google Maps or MapQuest. The next day as you're passing through the Quad Cities, a notification pops up on your phone to let you know one lane on I-80 is shut down near the Northwest Boulevard exit. It recommends you veer to the right, and hop on I-280 so you can avoid the congested traffic ahead.

Right now, your smartphone has all the data it needs to make this happen. What's missing is the ability for it to think ahead, anticipate your needs, and offer appropriate choices.

That's what the search for contextual intelligence is all about—training your phone to make suggestions in the proper context.

As I said earlier, your phone is the perfect stalker. It knows everything there is to know about you. It knows where you are, where you are going, and where you've been, because of its GPS location services. The truth is your smartphone knows more about you than your wife, your girlfriend, or your mother. The odds are, it knows more about you than you know about yourself.

Whether you know it or not, Google knows just about everything there is to know about you. They've been collecting information on your search history since the first day you logged onto their service.

You may have forgotten about that visit you made to an online dating site eleven years ago. The problem is, deleting a search doesn't make it go away. Google doesn't forget things that easily. They know about all those previous visits you made to the dark side of the web, and all those cars you looked at five years ago before you purchased your Mustang GT. Google remembers all of them and every dealer website you visited.

Google's *web and APP history* has been keeping tabs on all of us since 2005. They use the information they collect to build a profile about you. It keeps tabs on such things as your age, gender, interests, hobbies, quirks, and search results. This information is the basis for how they decide what comes next. It's how Google determines which search results it should display for you. For each of us, the results are different based on our past browsing history.

What most users don't understand is when you delete your browser history it doesn't erase the data stored on Google's servers. It just deletes the browser history stored locally on your device. That way your friends and family can't stalk you, but Google still can.

It's scary.

George Orwell's paranoid vision of *1984* is here. Only it isn't *Big Brother* who is watching us; it's *Big Data*.

Here's the deal.

Google, Apple, and Microsoft are all attempting to do the same thing. They're trying to get your device to learn enough about you so it can anticipate what you want to do next and provide the appropriate information, just as you need it. I think Rafe Needleman described it best in an article he authored for *Yahoo Tech*.[30] He said artificial intelligence would be somewhat like "autocorrect." Your smartphone will "autosuggest" what you should do next, based on your history. To do that, your smartphone would draw on your prior browsing history, and what it knows about you from your GPS location services, and your text messages, and emails.

The hard part is getting your phone to think contextually. As human beings, we can put things in context, based on what's happening now. As an example, let's say you're sitting in your house. You smell something burning and see smoke coming from the kitchen. The next thing you know the smoke alarm goes off. Most people can put two and two together to determine something is wrong, and understand that maybe the house is on

---

[30] Needleman, Rafe. *Why Artificial Intelligence Is Going to Look Like a Smartphone Keyboard.* Yahoo Tech. March 15, 2015.

fire. A normal person is either going to check it out, or dial 9-1-1, and run out of the house screaming "fire!"

Here's a tougher one.

Let's say; you have an appointment set to replace your windshield at 9:15. The Glass Barn texts you and says they're running an hour behind schedule. Is that okay? Or do you want to reschedule? That text is buried amongst several other messages. Most of them are junk. A coupon for a dollar off a sandwich, free drinks at the bar down the street, and a contest entry. Which messages should your phone hide, or display? Most people would say the message from the Glass Barn should be displayed first—because it's more urgent. But, how do you teach a chunk of metal and memory chips to make that decision? That's the real challenge.

When contextual intelligence works, it's amazing. The problem is, right now your phone gets it right less than a third of the time.

Google is working hard to improve on that number. Their future depends on getting it right. *Time Magazine* ran an article by Victor Lukerson a while back, titled, "Google Searches for Its Future."[31] The premise was it's a whole new world out there. Google became the "go to" search engine because of their excellence in desktop search, but mobile has changed everything. If Google wants to survive, they need to reinvent themselves. The

---

[31] Luckerson, Victor. *Google Searches for Its Future.* Time Tech. 2016.

**future is mobile**, and Google has determined the only way they can survive in this new reality is to focus in on "voice search" and "Google Now."

Here's how they intend to make good on that promise to reinvent themselves.

Google Now on Tap, the most recent version of Google Now is essentially high-tech spyware that keeps track of everything you do. It takes what it knows about you, such as your location at various times of the day. It then tries to anticipate what you will need to know at that moment and provide that information before you even know you need it.

To do this, Google Now on Tap takes espionage to the next level. It monitors your text messages, emails, and info displayed in your APPs. Google says the key to making Now on Tap work is "APP indexing." A study by Google[32] discovered the average smartphone user only uses 26 percent of the APPs on their phone. 25 percent of the APPs on their phones don't get used at all. APP indexing helps you to "re-engage your existing APPs through Google search."

The result is a more seamless user experience. The more you use your phone, the more it will learn about you, and the more accurate its predictions will be. If that isn't enough, Google has

---

[32] *App Indexing: Connect users to your app when they need it most.* Google. November 23, 2015.

over 100 billion web pages indexed. That gives them ready access to just about any information they need to make an informed decision.

Voice is the next part of the equation. Google wants to make your search experience hands free. You should be able to go to the grocery store after work and say, "Now, pull up my shopping list," and it should display your list. Your phone should also display a card containing the message your wife texted you earlier in the day on your way to work. "Don't forget the barbecue sauce and chips."

Google Now on Tap was designed to use natural language processing to give answers quickly and in the correct context.

Apple is shooting for a similar experience with their "Proactive" assistant. They began development of "Proactive" in 2013 with the goal of challenging Google Now. The program assembles information from messages, email, Passbook, calendar, contacts, and other third party APPs to make smart suggestions about what you should do next. It links with Siri so that users can speak their commands.

Apple's biggest advantage is Siri. Its voice capabilities and responses exceed anything Google can bring to the table. Siri has a well-developed personality. She can speak more naturally and respond in a more humanlike manner than Google's voice persona. Siri also has a great sense of humor, something Google can't match. Where Google excels is in its maps. Google Maps beats Apple Maps hands down. Because Google has an immense search history to draw on, in many cases their responses are more accurate and displayed in the proper context more often.

Over the next several years both services should become more accurate. Right now, it's a matter of building up more search history and training your device to connect the dots so it can offer up more relevant suggestions. The more your phone knows about you, the more likely it is to provide suggestions and solutions you can use.

The more pressing concern is, can we trust Apple or Google with all this information. Both services require you to opt in and give them explicit permission to spy on you.

Should you do it?

It's a personal decision only you can make. If you just use your phone to make phone calls and send an occasional text, you are probably safe opting out and withholding permissions. If you're a cell phone junkie, withholding permissions is going to dampen your search experience. Your phone is not going to be able to offer you smart suggestions to help you decide what comes next if you don't give it complete access to your device.

The only way you can have a truly smart phone is by granting it access to all your most private information.

# Beacons

**E**ssentially, a beacon is a radio transmitter that sends out a one-way signal. It operates on a (BLE) Bluetooth Low Energy frequency that transmits signals over a short distance, generally less than 1000 meters (roughly one-half a mile). A single watch sized battery can power a beacon for up to three years. The cost is so low that a five-year-old would get change back from his weekly allowance. Generic beacons sell on Amazon and eBay for roughly ten bucks. The real cost is in the software and programming required to operate the beacon. That can easily run into the thousands of dollars.

I like to think of a beacon as your basic couch potato. It sits there on the couch (or in most cases, stuck to a wall), and broadcasts signals to passing smartphones all day. If you're old enough to remember *Bewitched*, think of it as Gladys Kravitz poking her head out the window all day to spy on Darrin and Samantha Stephens. Beacons send out a signal every 350ms, or roughly several thousand times a second. When a beacon receives a signal back, it performs a preprogrammed action. Most often, it sends a text message to that device.

As I mentioned earlier, beacons only broadcast signals. They don't collect any information, so there's no danger of them snatching any personal information from a user's phone. But for a beacon to work, several things need to happen. Users need to download the corresponding APP, open it up when they're on location, and enable Bluetooth service on their device.

That's one of the things beacon technology has going for it. People feel safe using it because they are in total control. You only receive messages if you opt into the APP. After you've opted into the APP, you're still in control. If you receive too many messages or a string of irrelevant messages, you can remove the APP from your device, or turn off your Bluetooth. As soon as you do that, the notifications stop.

Right now, retailers are the biggest users of beacons. *Entrepreneur Magazine*[33] reports 4.5 million beacons will be in use by 2018, 3.5 million are expected to be in use in brick-and-mortar stores.

Here's why beacons are such a big deal.

---

[33] Belicove, Mikal. *Everything Business Owners Need to Know About Beacons.* Entrepreneur Magazine. April 17, 2015.

*Entrepreneur Magazine* reports big retailers, like Macy's and McDonald's, are seeing 60 percent engagement rates—and 30 percent purchase rates when they employ beacon technology.

That's insane!

When a company invests megabucks in a direct mail campaign, they consider themselves fortunate if they get a one or two percent response rate. Radio, TV, and newspaper ads are all a crapshoot. Unless you include a coupon, it's next to impossible to measure their effectiveness. Beacon technology provides instant gratification to organizations that use it. You switch it on, and consumers walk in to take advantage of your offer.

**Although beacon technology** has been around for several years, mainstream businesses have been slow to jump on the beacon bandwagon.

Target began to test beacon technology in their stores in August of 2015. What sets them apart is they were totally transparent in the way they approached it. They published an article in their store newsletter, *A Bullseye View*,[34] that explained the technology, and how they intended to use it.

Moreover, they made it sound like an epic win for customers. It's "their latest move to create a smarter, more convenient, and

---

[34] *Testing, Testing, 1, 2, 3: Beacon Technology Arrives in 50 Target Stores*. A Bullseye View. August 5, 2015.

inspiring in-store shopping experience." Target told customers the APP would let them know about "timely deals and recommendations."

After that, the article invited customers to join the adventure. To get started, they just needed to download the Target smartphone APP and enable Bluetooth on their phones.

Most retailers would have left it at that. Target took things a step further to ensure customers would feel comfortable when they used the new technology. They provided detailed screen shots that showed APP users the types of messages they could expect to receive. Target also made shoppers a promise they would not abuse the technology. They assured shoppers they would limit the number of notifications they would receive to no more than two per trip.

It was a smart move. It educated shoppers and encouraged them to make the leap and try out the new technology. And, unlike many stores that try to jumpstart a new shopping program or APP, Target didn't resort to offering bribes or freebies to entice users to opt in. Instead, they engaged with users personally through targeted content marketing.

**McDonald's tested beacon technology** in 26 of their Columbus, Georgia locations in late 2015. During the four weeks, they ran the trial; McChicken sandwich sales increased 8 percent over the previous month, and sales of Chicken McNuggets jumped 7.5 percent. *Mobile Commerce Daily*[35] reported McDonald's received 18,000 offer redemptions during that period.

No matter how you slice it, that's a lot of chicken!

The way the program worked, customers who had the APP downloaded to their phones received SMS messages that contained surveys, coupons, and alerts when they walked into the locations.

During the most recent promotions, the offers were targeted to move chicken. But in the future, as beacon technology advances, what would happen if the McDonald's APP stored a user's purchase history, and when the beacon received a signal back, it could pull up your individual history, and send out a personalized offer? How effective would that be? Would offer redemption jump from 20 percent to 50 percent, or more? That's one of the things that makes beacon technology so exciting. It's still in its infancy, and it's receiving stellar results. Who can say what the future will bring?

McDonald's could send out alerts to let customers know the McRib is back, or the Shamrock Shake has returned for a limited engagement.

---

[35] Bohannon, Caitlyn. *McDonald's beacons reap 18,000 redemption offers.* Mobile Commerce Daily. December 19, 2014.

McDonald's recently ran a beacon powered promo in several Turkish locations. They offered McDonald's Café users a *Buy One, Get One* free offer on select coffees. To get the offer, shoppers had to have the *Shopping Genie* APP downloaded to their devices. The results were astounding. *Kontaxt.io*[36] reported 20 percent of McDonald's visitors took advantage of the offer, and 30 percent of them used it more than once.

What that means for restaurants, and savvy retailers, is customers are more than willing to engage with you—if the offer is right for them. Over the next few years, as retailers test and refine beacon technology they will be able to present custom offers tailored to individual customers. Let's say you eat at Subway every Wednesday, and order a ham and cheese sandwich with extra mayo and Swiss cheese, and on Friday you order a turkey sandwich, small drink, and chips, Subway would be able to send you a coupon as you approach the location. Or, they could try to upsell you, and offer a dollar off the foot long, instead of the regular sandwich.

Whatever happens, it's all about personalizing the offer, and not abusing your customer relationship. Beacons are an opt-in technology. If marketers go overboard or make irrelevant offers, customers will most likely opt out.

---

[36] *Context Converts: McDonald's Drives Conversion Rate in Store of 20% With Context-Sensitive Offers Powered by Kontaxt.io*. Kontaxt.io Blog. April 28, 2015.

**There's no escaping the fact**; your phone is going to bring you more personalized offers.

*Imagine a family trip to the mall in the not too distant future.*

*As soon as you enter the mall, you receive a welcome message. Minutes later you receive an invitation to visit the newest stores to enter their lineup or check out the sports card show in the center of the mall. After you've been walking around the mall for a while, you catch the aroma of pizza and popcorn coming from the food court. Next thing you know, you receive a text message from Papa Joe's Pizza offering you a free soda when you purchase two slices of pizza, or a pitcher of soft drinks when you purchase a family size pizza. You hadn't planned to eat at the mall, but the price is right. The smell is enticing. The family grabs a seat while dad picks up the order.*

*Fifteen minutes later, just as you're finishing up your meal, you receive another text. This one is from the bookstore. It offers you 25 percent off the latest James Patterson thriller. Your daughter receives a similar offer for $5.00 off a new blouse at Little Miss. After dinner, you split up, and head off on your separate ways, agreeing to meet up at the front door in a half hour. Of course, the kids are late as usual, so you text them, to let them know it's time to go.*

*As you're leaving, you receive another message. It thanks you for stopping by and offers you a $10.00 discount if you return within the next five days. You normally only shop at the mall two or three times a year, but you decide not to delete that text. Instead of picking up dog food at Walmart next week when you do your regular grocery shopping, maybe you'll get it at the Pet Emporium in the mall.*

Sound far-fetched?

The technology needed to power this scenario has been available for several years. The only difference is more businesses are experimenting with beacon technology. It gives restaurants and retailers an amazing opportunity to tailor special offers to potential patrons, as soon as they enter, or approach their establishments. Doctors, dentists, and other medical professionals can use the technology to check in, or greet patients and businesses and schools can use the technology to track who's on site.

**Beacon technology offers** an incredible opportunity for nonprofits to take their customer service to the next level.

Let's take a trip to the connected museum.

*Your tour bus pulls up to the Putnam Museum in Davenport, Iowa. As you file into the museum, the ticket clerk reminds you to download the museum APP to your phone. Shortly after you download the APP, you receive a message that welcomes you to the museum. It includes a list of major exhibits, a floorplan, with arrows pointing to the restrooms, and other useful information.*

*As you reach the local history corridor, you receive several short messages that describe some of the displays in more detail. During the nature walk, a text gives you more details about the polar bear exhibit, the zebras, and it challenges you to locate the warthog hidden in the far-right corner of the wildlife display.*

*Downstairs in the* Hall of Egypt, *you receive a message that details the discovery of the two mummies exhibited there. As you make your way back upstairs you receive a reminder—the new Imax movie begins in fifteen minutes. Be sure to grab your tickets, if you plan to attend the performance.*

*As you walk out of the museum, a final message reminds you to visit the gift shop and pick up a souvenir. And then, just as you're walking out the door, you receive a coupon for a discount admission to the Figge Art Museum located just a short distance away.*

Very few, if any, museums do this today, but the technology to make such a visit possible is available. Every local museum, or historical society, could implement a similar program. Cities could set up a series of transmitters to power a local history walk. Every time someone who has the APP downloaded to their device comes within range, they would receive a text about the house or business they are approaching.

For you, the consumer, beacon technology can save you money, and help to prevent frustration. But, if you're annoyed by all those messages, and just want to make them go away, there is a simple solution. You can turn off all the notifications. Since they only come through APPs you have downloaded to your phone; you can delete the APP, or change its settings. On an iPhone, you would go into your *APP Settings > Privacy > Location Service* and disable it. On an Android device, you would > open the *APP Drawer* > scroll down to *Location*, and tap it > scroll down to *Google Location Settings* and tap it > tap on *Location Reporting*, and slide it over to off (to turn off *Location History*, slide the switch to off). Or, a simpler solution, would be to turn off your Bluetooth when you feel overwhelmed with the SMS messages you receive.

# Security

**Very few cell phone owners** take precautions to secure their devices from data intrusions. That's going to change. Android users, especially, are going to need to install virus protection software. That should come as no surprise to anyone who's used a PC. Steve Manzuik, director of security research at Duo Security cautions, "smartphones are essentially miniature computers that we carry in our pockets, and they have just as many potential security risks as a laptop or PC."

The other thing to remember is if you're like most people, you keep your life on your phone—photos, documents, notes, credit cards, bank account info, and even a catalog of all your passwords. If someone highjacks or steals your phone, they can break the bank, and take you for every penny you've got.

Here's something else to consider. If you don't have all that information backed up to a cloud, or a hard drive, it's gone. Sure, you can get some of it back by chasing down bank statements and such, but your pictures, music, and password file—they're gone. Kaput. Finished.

"Smartphones are becoming a necessity in our lives," says Walter O'Brien, founder, and CEO of *Scorpion Computer Services, Inc*. "Most smartphone users don't know that there are security options on their smartphones. But several built-in security features exist to help consumers protect their smartphones and the valuable [information stored] on them.

"There are minimal steps consumers should always take:

"Keep your phone's software updated. You'll receive update notifications through your phone, and often-times those updates include security patches. Frequently those patches fix security vulnerabilities those firms like Scorpion Computer Services find on behalf of telecom providers. It's important to update your phone when you receive those notifications.

"Turn off your Wi-Fi and Bluetooth when you're not using them," says O'Brien. "A favorite route that hackers use to crack into smartphones is through wireless. With two phones—one acting as a GSM modem for a laptop—it's possible to use a second phone to receive information from your hacked phone. You can get raided in the middle of the night and not know it until the morning when you learn that your private information has been accessed or copied."

**"Physical security remains** the top risk for smartphone users," warns Ken Smith, of Secure State. "A lot of people may believe that hacking involves highly technical methods that the average person may not be able to detect. But simple things, like physically securing [your phone] to prevent it from being lost or stolen" can be effective in many situations. He also emphasizes, "PINs aren't as much of a deterrent as some people may think. Once, during a vulnerability assessment at a corporation, we found a smartphone sitting in someone's car. The access method was a lock screen pattern. We were able to get into the phone simply from the oil residue left behind by the user putting the pattern in."

Simply put, if a hacker, or thief, wants to get into your phone, you can't stop them. All you can do is slow them down, and make it more difficult for them to gain access to your data. As Smith pointed out, sometimes thieves gain access because of the stupidest things—who would ever guess the grease residues left by your fingers could help a thief gain access to your device?

Things happen. Phones get lost or stolen. It's a fact of life. One of the things I asked Walter O'Brien was what's the one thing smartphone users can do to protect themselves in this eventuality. He said, "The best practices are to use a biometric authentication to access your phone, whether that is facial recognition or a finger swipe. Most smartphones now have built-in authentication. For those that don't have biometric authentication available, use the simple key code lock feature. In most instances, the next person to find your lost phone isn't going to be an expert hacker. Do take advantage of the ability your device has to remotely 'Wipe' or erase the device. Both Android and iPhone devices can be configured in preparation for the eventuality."

If you don't do anything else, set up a pin number to access your device, and enable a fingerprint sensor (if available). These two things will protect your information from most thieves and hackers.

A lot of times, it's the things we do or don't do, that put our phones at risk. "Phones that are not kept up-to-date should be considered at risk," says Steve Manzuik. When you receive a notification that an update is ready, you should download and install it as soon as possible. He also cautions us that "users who jailbreak, or root their devices, and then use alternate APP markets, or even pirated APPs, are obviously at a higher risk of malware infections and other attacks."

"Antivirus software is just one part of a broader suite of protective software that you'll want on your smartphone," says Walter O'Brien. "The biggest risk is someone physically accessing your phone because you set it down or lost it, and you didn't add authentication to allow access to your phone so a thief can just start browsing your personal information. Viruses, malware, and ransomware all exist for smartphones, too, and, while less likely to affect a given consumer; they'll still want to make sure they're protected against it. Android's security software measures are significant. That's why the most important thing a consumer can do is to update their phones when security patches are available."

"Historically, Android users are more at risk," says Ken Smith. "This has to do with the lack of control Android has because there are multiple manufacturers of devices as well as a wider array of APP writers. Apple controls the manufacturing of their devices," so there are fewer opportunities to hack into their operating system.

However, Calon Alpar cautions us Apple phones aren't as secure as we've been led to believe. Alpar says, at the very least, you need to "update your phone's OS [operating system] and APPs."

"Apple has always considered IOS safe," he says, "but just in 2015, they were exposed to some huge attacks. InsOmnia, Xcode Ghost, and YiSpecter all exposed IOS in a new way." It's just the beginning for attacks on IOS. "A remote jailbreak was found possible on IOS. This was a game changer as jailbreaking a device is always thought of as needing a USB connection." Now, it's possible for a hacker to "take complete control of your device, just by the user unknowingly opening a link on the mobile browser."

Walter O'Brien also warns us about a new threat on the horizon for smartphone users. He says, "Ransomware is becoming an increasingly popular way for people to steal from unsuspecting consumers. Ransomware locks down your hard drive and demands payment to release a key to restore or access your files. At Scorpion Computer Services, we've seen reports of ransoms demanded in the amount of just a few dollars on up into the thousands. The victim has a limited amount of time to make payment in order to restore his files. It's unfortunately very effective."

**Right now, there are any number** of crazy threats emanating from scammers in Jamaica and Nigeria. The funny thing is, these are all low-tech scams that don't have anything to do with the internet.

Here's a typical pitch from a scammer.

"Congratulations, Mrs. Gullible Sucker. You just won the Publisher's Clearinghouse Sweepstakes. To secure your prize, we just need to collect a good faith deposit." (Or, they may say, all they need to do is "collect your financial information," and your prize will be on its way).

Do you remember the old saying, "A sucker and his money are soon parted?"

If you share any of your financial information with these guys or send them any money, they're going to clean you out.

Here's another piece of advice. If you see a number you don't recognize on your call list, don't press redial. Scammers use toll-free numbers that redirect to foreign countries. If you press redial, your cellular carrier is going to hit you with international charges.

The same advice goes for your email. If you receive an email from someone you don't recognize, don't open it. And, whatever you do, don't click on unknown links. That's how viruses get spread.

The key to securing your phone is to think before you act. Remember what we tell our kids about "stranger danger." That advice pertains as much to your cell phone, as it does to your kids. If you don't recognize a phone number that's calling you, don't answer your phone. And, whatever you do, don't press redial. If you receive an email from someone you don't know, don't open it. Don't click on links you receive in emails, or on social media sites. And, if you get a pop-up asking you to check your phone for viruses, you can bet your ass it's a scam. Close your browser immediately and reopen it.

**Could we be faced with the possibility** of "death by a hacker." Author Robert Siciliano suggests with the, "increasing advances in the realm of IoT, hacking can become a life-and-death matter, not just the nuisance of some baby monitor getting hacked, and the hacker spewing out lewd comments for mommy to hear. For instance, it's only a matter of time before a doctor, hundreds of miles away, remotely control a patient's implanted heart arrhythmia controller.

"What if a hacker gains access and demands ransom or else?"

The IoT creates life-threatening dangers we don't see with smartphones. What happens if someone hacks in while a doctor is performing a medical procedure, or what if someone shuts down a pacemaker?

How do we prevent medical hacking?

Frank Spano, Executive Director, and Founder of *the Counter Terrorism Institute* cautions. "New risks, threats, and vulnerabilities will continue to develop [and] this is perhaps most apparent in the ever-expanding world that is the Internet of Things (IoT), where consumer reliance, software holes, and limited digital security infrastructure combine to provide a hotbed for hackers, terrorists, and other cyber-criminals. A good rule of thumb is that the more interconnected technology becomes (spanning multiple service providers, networks, and hardware manufacturers) the more vulnerable the entire IoT web becomes."

His suggestion is that each of us needs to take "ownership" of our technology products. Spano cautions users that "digital security" includes more than deploying "antivirus software or a firewall." He says, "businesses and individuals need to be aware that - especially in IoT technology - the enemy exists in far more than just electrons and code. Instead, today's threats rely on a combination of digital and real-time intelligence collection and penetration techniques. To combat this, users of all kind should focus on increasing their awareness of the physical and digital world around them, identify and periodically assess their risks and vulnerabilities, and adopt a personal defense mindset that includes efforts to safeguard personal data, passwords and access codes, schedules, identifying information, and even things as seemingly mundane as game console login details."

The *Connected Car* presents similar issues. Terrorists could create havoc by hacking into a traffic grid and shutting down stop lights. Worse yet, they could hack into your car's computer system and shut it down, or slam on the brakes creating pandemonium on the highways.

Why should terrorists use guns, when they can inflict more damage without ever leaving home?

Cellular security is an issue that needs to be tackled today before terrorists turn the internet against us. Five years from now the damage will already be done.

# Mobilegeddon

**W**hat's your worst mobile experience? Trying to read text so small you need a triple strength magnifying glass to make it out? Scrolling your screen back and forth so that you can read a string of run-on text? Or, zooming your screen to make individual links clickable? I mean, I've got fat fingers. It drives me nuts whenever I try to click on mobile links. I'm not going to do it. When it's time to start clicking links, I make the switch to a tablet or laptop.

*Mobilegeddon* is Google's way of signaling they get it. Mobile is here to stay. On any given day, fifty percent of internet searches originate from smartphones, and Google knows—that number is only going to grow.

Website developers were ruing the day—April 21$^{st}$, 2015. That's the day *Mobilegeddon* went live. Many website developers expected a replay of the Y2K crisis. Fears ran high that popular websites would disappear from search entirely. When that didn't happen immediately, developers shrugged it off, as another threat without teeth, but two months later *Mobilegeddon* reared its ugly head, and many well-placed websites tumbled in the rankings. The threat was real. It just took time for the reality to click in.

Essentially, *Mobilegeddon* ensures a more user-friendly smartphone experience. It requires website and APP developers to do four things.

1. Create programs in software commonly found on mobile devices.
2. Make text readable, without forcing users to zoom in on it.
3. Eliminate horizontal scrolling.
4. Provide large, easy to click links.

Another change, effective as of November of 2015, punishes websites that take over a user's screen to push an APP. Google decided the practice frustrated smartphone users and provided for a bad experience. Web sites that continue to steal screens are subject to removal from mobile search.

Why is this important?

Over two-thirds of web searches in the United States originate on Google. On any given day, over fifty percent of searches get launched from smartphones. If your website gets demoted in search, your business is going to take a hit.

Here are a couple of key facts to keep in mind about *Mobilegeddon*.

1. It only affects searches made from smartphones. Searches conducted from PCs, laptops, and tablets are not affected.
2. Google doesn't just arbitrarily choose which sites get punished. On any given day, tens of millions of tiny Google bots crawl the internet to search for websites that don't comply with *Mobilegeddon*.
3. Google gave developers two months to rearrange their sites to make them compliant with *Mobilegeddon*. If they failed to take action, they knew what they could expect.

And, if you have any doubts whether Mobilegeddon is working, consider this. *seoClarity*[37] reports since the inception of Mobilegeddon, there is a 69 percent difference in the results shown for desktop, and for mobile searches. Another interesting trend noted in many recent studies indicates Google is making a killing from the fallout caused by *Mobilegeddon*. A recent study published by *Adobe*,[38] says Pay-Per-Click (PPC) advertising is up

---

[37] Heuser, Ryan. *Mobilegeddon: Here Is What's Happening Now.* seoClarity. April 30, 2015.
[38] *Digital Advertising Report.* Adobe Digital Index. Q2 2015.

significantly since the change, as websites demoted in search throw money at Google to keep their sites in front of browsers.

Whatever else can be said, *Mobilegeddon* is one of the best things to happen to smartphone users. It eliminates clunky, slow moving, ad ridden mobile sites, and ensures smartphone users receive a faster, more relevant browsing experience.

# 5G - the Future of Cellular

**4G, LTE, LTE-A, and 5G. What are they?** What do they mean? How are they going to change the way we consume data?

Long Term Evolution-Advanced (LTE-A) is what LTE is supposed to be. When fully deployed, it should increase network speed by two to three times over what it is today. Because of its increased latency, there should also be fewer dropped connections.

Right now, peak 4G data speeds approach 100 megabits per second when moving—such as in a car, train, or walking. By 4G standards, that speed should be closer to 1 gigabyte.

What gives?

Perhaps the best way to understand LTE speed limits is to examine how LTE-A works.

LTE-A is a mix of three different technologies—carrier aggregation, MIMO (multiple input – multiple output), and relay nodes.

Essentially, carrier aggregation combines the bandwidth of multiple connections into one single connection. In theory, up to five bands can be aggregated together. In reality—three is the maximum; two is the norm.

MIMO harnesses radio signal problems. It's somewhat like when you're listening to the radio. Some stations tend to overlap, or the signal appears to fade in and out. MIMO combines the signal from multiple stations to make them stronger. The result is a faster connection.

Relay nodes are somewhat like microcells. They're mini power boosters that allow your smartphone to use several cellular signals at once.

Here's how it all comes together.

Transmission speeds are affected by how many people are using the tower, and how many people are on the network. 300 Mbps speeds are possible, but 150 Mbps is more likely the peak speed you will ever receive. Between 5 to 12 Mbps is what you can expect to receive, and for most uses it is sufficient. There are many reasons 4G doesn't achieve its peak potential. Some of the stumbling blocks include—buildings, trees, and other wifi signals.

Way back—in the dark ages of LTE; a 2013 survey showed AT&T had the fastest LTE network. Verizon placed second, followed by Sprint, then T-Mobile.[39] However—LTE speeds vary, based on your location. AT&T may be number one nationwide, but for individual users—it's all about where you're at—NOW. Davenport, Iowa may have cellular speeds of twice that found in Bangor, Maine, but someone in Bangor, Maine, may experience speeds three times faster than someone located in Boise, Idaho. It depends on the signal available where you are.

Verizon advertises it has the largest LTE-A network.

T-Mobile says that's nothing to brag about.

"Really. LTE-Advanced," exclaimed Neville Ray, Chief Technology Officer at T-Mobile. "That same technology (2 channel carrier aggregation) has been available to T-Mobile customers since 2014...Look, in reality, carrier aggregation is not new. It's so 2014."[40]

Verizon defended itself, saying wireless speed isn't as important as the size of the network. In their view, more is better. And, what they have now is good enough for most of their subscribers. Consistent speeds are what Verizon feels is important—even more so than superfast speeds. Buffering and drops are what ruin the experience for cellular users.

---

[39] Sullivan, Mark. "Tech hive's Wireless Week: Testing America's Networks." PC World. May 20, 2013.

[40] Ray, Neville. "LTE Advanced Is So 2014. We're already on to the next big thing. Verizon is 50% Faster...and still slower than T-Mobile!" T-Mobile Media Relations Home. September 6, 2016.

**Faster data is what everyone wants.**

Right now, smartphone users with 4G LTE consume four times as much data as those without it. By 2020 the average smartphone user is expected to consume 4.4 megabytes of data a month. Tablet data use is expected to increase at an eight-fold rate from 2015 to 2020. Or, if you prefer to look at data consumption by the cellular market as a whole—it is expected to increase from 2.5 exabytes per month to 23.34 exabytes per month by 2019.[41]

Most of that increase will be due to increased video consumption. The expectation is 72 percent of data will be consumed watching video on YouTube, Netflix, Facebook, and other video platforms.

5G is one of the newer technologies that will make this all possible. Most experts expect 5G to be 40 to 100 times faster than current data transmission speeds using LTE and LTE-A.

There's a lot of talk about 5G, and how it's going to transform our mobile experiences. Many magazines, white papers, and news reporters have hailed 5G as the second coming, or as the beginning of a new age in cellular technology.

It may well be.

But, people need to understand—5G is currently just a jumble of words. AT&T, Verizon, and T-Mobile all have a different vision

---

[41] Cisco Visual Networking Index. February 2016.

for what they expect the service to be. Some experts insist 5G is nothing more than a label for advanced 4G, or LTE-A.

*PC Magazine* suggests the first use for 5G will be in home networking. They say AT&T is talking about using "5G to replace its old DSL offerings, letting the company deliver a 'quad-play' of Direct TV service, 5G home internet, wireless phone, and home phone." Verizon has something similar in mind. Their first deployment of 5G is expected to involve home internet services.[42]

"Some of the early customer-realized service offerings will be for home-based fixed wireless networks," says Wayne Smith. "Carriers will want to replace their antiquated DSL offering. In both cases, these fixed wireless offerings would be as [*PC Magazine*] said 'quad play' for Internet, TV, home phone, security. This was attempted in mid-90's with MMDS."

"5G is the next major phase of wireless mobile technology," says Gray Hancock. "We are currently in 4G / LTE (Long Term Evolution) and have been for only a few years. 5G will let us use a platform that will manage internet, security, smart appliances and TV, replacing antiquated landline services such as DSL. Wireless service carriers will most likely use small cells that exist on towers and advanced antenna technologies to boost the signals."

---

[42] "What is 5G?" by Sascha Segan. PC Magazine. June 21, 2016.

**That still leaves the big question.**

What is 5G?

The biggest thing you need to know about 5G is that it doesn't exist—Not yet, anyway. Everyone is working to define it. But right now, it's just an amalgamation of ideas fluttering around in people's heads.

- 5G is all about small, compact cell technology.
- 5G will most likely be an extension of 4G LTE technology. They will work together, side by side, providing a faster, more robust cellular network.
- 5G is all about the Internet of Things (IOT). For smartphone users, it's all about faster speeds, and higher quality streaming videos. But, that same speed is just as important to the IOT—where machines need data ASAP—to function properly.
- 5G is crucial to the development of self-driving cars. They "require the one millisecond delay time provided in the 5G specification."[43]

---

[43] "Understanding 5G: Perspectives on Future Technological Advancements in Mobile." GSMA Intelligence. December 2014. (pages 9-10).

**For now, and into the foreseeable future**, 4G and LTE-A are where the action is.

Even when 5G gets fully implemented, 4G LTE will continue to carry the bulk of the network traffic—especially out in the open, and in rural areas where the small cell technology required to power 5G won't exist.

One of the most asked questions is, when will we see 5G technology? *GSMA Intelligence* published the best response to that. "When 5G arrives will be determined by what 5G turns out to be."[44] They say, "LTE is still in the early stage of its lifecycle." Historically cellular technologies have a twenty-year lifespan. LTE got its start in 2009. If they're right, that means LTE will likely play a major role in cellular technology until at least 2030. The key takeaway is: 4G LTE won't remain static. It will evolve as needed to complement and enhance the 5G network.

"5G is currently in a technology and specifications development stage," says Wayne Smith. "This stage will soon produce a set of standards that manufacturers will use to develop the technologies. It is important to note this process is a collaborative process composed of key manufacturers, nations, network providers, standards organizations, etc."

---

[44] "Understanding 5G: Perspectives on Future Technological Advancements in Mobile." GSMA Intelligence. December 2014. (page 15).

"5G will be a service above 4G at some point in time. However, at this time it is simply a technology waiting for network infrastructure to support it," says Gray Hancock. "Standards must be developed and agreed upon for interconnectivity with all wireless carriers. As far as testing, this is happening in test beds all over the world. There are 21 sites where companies and perceived partners are testing the technology and commitment to the perceived benefits."

Cell phone technology—G (or 1G) got its start in the early 1990's. 2G made it possible for users to send text messages between two wireless phones. 3G brought it all together, and allowed smartphone users to talk, text, and browse the internet. 4G came along as an improvement to 3G—it allowed smartphone users to upload and download large data files seamlessly—think iTunes and Netflix.

Previous technologies relied on large cellular towers that could transmit signals over long distances. 5G is going to be an entirely different animal altogether. It's going to rely on millions of small microcells that can broadcast for a maximum of three to five blocks—not ten to twenty miles.

That's where a lot of the confusion lies.

The current 4G network can't handle all the gizmo's, gadget's, and whatchamacallits we're throwing at it. 5G can relieve some of the pressure the IoT, smart cars, connected houses, and such are putting on the network.

5G is one answer—but it's not the final solution. It's one piece of the puzzle.

As I already mentioned, 5G is going to revolutionize home networking. It's going to do away with dead zones, dropped wifi signals, video buffering, and a whole slew of other networking problems. It's going to change the shape of things. Instead of having one modem and router in your home, you're likely to have many.

For businesses, 5G will eliminate Ethernet cables. It will speed up data transmission. It will enable advanced robotics, sensors, switches, and other components of the IoT. Without 5G, self-driving cars will be pushed farther out into the future.

5G will very likely open up a free for all in the home internet market as cellular carriers' scramble to offer truly unlimited data for home use. Up to now, cellular carriers have been edged out of the market, because they didn't have the capacity to challenge cable companies. 5G is going to change all that by providing inexpensive, unlimited data—everywhere.

It should be a win-win for everyone.

**5G is going to provide** wireless users with a more seamless experience.

It's going to be the next step in internet connectivity. 4K and Ultra HD videos will stream quicker. Connected cars and other devices will be able to connect to the network effortlessly. It is expected to be backward compatible with 4G and 3G, but the bad news is—your current device isn't going to cut it. It will require new devices to connect to the 5G network.

The signal frequency for 4G ranges up to 20MHZ. 5G will occupy the air space up to 6 GHZ.

That's good and bad.

That frequency is currently unused. That means fewer interruptions and faster transmission speeds should be possible. The biggest problem is higher frequency signals have a shorter transmission range. Instead of shooting out a signal for miles and miles. 5G is a more compact solution. It will cover a three to five block area. Because of this, MIMO is necessary to boost the signal.

To make 5G work will require one small cell, or microcell, for every twelve to twenty homes. That means carriers are in for a major buildout to put the new service into operation. Business buildings and private homes are going to need to join the party, and become part of the small cell network. Small cells would need to be mounted to rooftops, lamp poles, street signs, and hundreds of other unique locations.

5G is also going to require all new phones. One piece of the puzzle is a new chipset. 5G devices will require smaller microchips that use less power, so they don't burn your battery out as fast. The chipset is also expected to be overlaid with micro antennas to increase reception.

Government cooperation is going to be essential to making 5G a reality.

In his 2016 State of the Union address, European Union President, Jean-Claude Juncker, made it a top priority to install **free public wifi** throughout the European Union before 2020.

Juncker said, "We need to be connected. Our economy needs it. People need it. And we have to invest in that connectivity now."[45]

Here's a breakdown of the rollout from a European Union press release.

- Schools, universities, and public services should have one-gigabyte service.
- All households should have a minimum of 100 Mbps service.
- All urban areas should have "uninterrupted 5G coverage." 5G service should be "commercially available in at least one major city in each EU member state by 2020."[46]

---

[45] State of the Union Address, 2016. European Union President, Jean-Claude Juncker.
[46] European Union Press Release. September 14, 2016.

**Here's the reality**.

5G isn't going to happen overnight. The International Telecommunications Union (ITU) has been trying to nail down the definition of 5G since 2012.

They haven't defined it yet, so what 5G will eventually become is anyone's guess.

My thought is it's going to be more like wifi on steroids than cellular. Most likely, the two services will blend so well; we won't be able to distinguish one from the other. "Not all 5G technologies are new," says Wayne Smith. "Many are technologies that are being implemented in the 4G networks. Remember, all technology stands on the foundations built in the past."

My thought is at some point we will no longer be tied to just one carrier. Most likely; everything will become interconnected. Our carrier will be determined more by where we are—than who we choose.

Gray Hancock isn't so sure about that. He says, "we will always be tied to a single service provider. The nascent stages of digital wireless carriers didn't have as much coverage as today. Carriers established reciprocal billing agreements for areas of non-coverage. Earlier on, each account had an associated area of operation within the existing network architecture. For example, if you are a Sprint customer and you drove out of the Sprint coverage area and into a Verizon area, Sprint's roaming agreement with Verizon would allow you to stay on the Sprint network and simply incur 'roaming' charges. Today, the network architecture is much different, largely due to data [the fact] can be delivered through the wireless carrier's nationwide data network.

"So, not to say never, but, users still need to have an account with one carrier for billing, device charges, long-term agreements/contracts, plus due to the impact of the 'cloud' on the overall network architecture."

**5G will create a new world of possibilities**, but probably not until 2025—or beyond.

# What's Next

SYL Chao is sure "Nothing will replace the smartphone, as the smartphone will reinvent itself every decade until artificial consciousness machines are available. Quantum phones might be next, as soon as current research in the Quantum Computing field mature, but then it will be the servers that lead its usage, followed by mobile devices." When asked about chip implants, he doesn't "see [them] coming to fruition within the [next] two decades."

**George Gracin III** thinks "one of the main reasons smartphones are taking over, could be because of the instant gratification we get from using them. It's so simple now. Pull it out of your pocket, [and] get instant access to the internet. The difference now is that as smartphones are becoming so powerful, with added mobile-optimized APPs and websites, they have become the replacement of people's computers completely."

**Anne Balduzzi** says, "Mobile devices will convert the act of meeting strangers into heartfelt handshakes or even hugs. Our phones will privately let us know what in-depth areas we share in common with people we pass or meet (e.g., same disease, same hobby, same life experiences, etc.) and enable us to dive deep into a conversation. We will also be able to point our devices at a location (shop, restaurant, nightclub) to determine if it fits with our style, allergies, or taste in food and music."

She goes on to say, "the notification will start by integrating with watches (possible now), so your wristband vibrates when you shake hands with someone with common threads. This will evolve and eventually be integrated into clothing, glasses, jewelry. So your earring may vibrate if someone nearby has a great story you should hear and you can check your watch or glasses for more details."

**Christopher Sharp** suggests, that "to see the future of cellular technology all you need to do is look at its past. The rate of advancement is predictable based on the time and distance between each high point the industry has accomplished. From the pager to the smartphone, to the autonomous car, the space between each advancement is decreasing rapidly. The personal jet pack of *The Jetsons* is now a reality, and the future is coming faster than ever before. Soon, cars will all be interconnected, and highways will be 'smart.' Your personal device will no longer be called a phone and will be able to call other people on its own, make reservations, and check the score of the game for you, and then report back."

**Ben Lee** says. "As devices integrate into our daily lives and workflow, wearables will make it easier and easier to stay in sync across all our devices - and that means eventually, smartphones will be obsolete. Whether it's a watch, pair of smart glasses, or an implanted microchip, future generations will be calling us dinosaurs when they see pictures of big, modern day smartphones - let alone the flip phones of only a few years ago!"

**Nolan Kier** says "the current trend of many cell phone designs points towards a simplistic, clean combined aesthetic and functionality component. Many developers are producing software and physical design functionality that emphasizes taking the 'guess work' out of the user experience. Despite the slightly steeper learning curve that is typically attributed to many Android devices due to preferences made apparent by their user base, many non-iOS devices like the NEXUS 6P exhibit signs of a sneak interface that prioritizes front-end simplicity coupled with back-end complexity. This 'behind the scenes' work is being implemented in many mobile devices across the board, including in Apple's newest iPhone designs where a user can utilize the phone's application processes in so few steps that it makes you wonder how they 'hid the wires.'

"For physical design, I think we can expect to see less and less sharp, geometric designs in favor of more fluid, shapely features that feel more natural to handle and carry. Much the same way many auto enthusiasts tend to rid their cars of excess emblems and trimmings, I think we will see a push towards limiting the number of physical features like buttons. Apple is currently leading the way in this design push, as rumors have hinted at research aimed at increasing the viability of wireless headphone use and charging, to eliminate the charging and audio ports."

**C. J. McElveen** says, "I believe that the mobile industry will continue to develop into monthly prepaid plans. Convenience is king when it comes to consumers, and it seems as though the major mobile companies are catching on. Most are offering prepaid or pay-per-use plans that allow consumers to decide how much they want to use and pay, allowing the consumers to be in control."

**Dennis Duty** says, "You can expect next-gen phones to have multiple cameras on the same face. This will allow for more accurate facial and gesture detection. Now that Nintendo's 3DS has perfected handheld 3d technology, we might even see similar tech used in our phones.

"We're going to see a revival of physical buttons on smartphones. Touchscreens are great, but they're not perfect for every situation. As more blue-collar and craftsmen upgrade their phones, more durable and tactile options will be the most appealing option."

**Dane Theisen** thinks, "Wearable technology is an emerging trend that can drastically change how consumers interact with cell phones. In the not so distant feature, handheld cellphones will become obsolete. Cell phones will eventually be embedded behind the user's ear, and will be integrated with the human body to provide benefits such as health monitoring."

**Austin Smith** says, "As devices integrate into our daily lives and workflow, wearables will make it easier and easier to stay in sync across all our devices - and that means that eventually, smartphones will be obsolete. Whether it's a watch, pair of smart glasses, or an implanted microchip, future generations will be calling us dinosaurs when they see pictures of big, modern day smartphones - let alone the flip phones of only a few years ago!"

**Kelly Graver** thinks, "Smartphone technology is reaching an exciting point now that they are nearly ubiquitous and are becoming the main platform for surfing the internet. The latest phones are nearly as powerful as desktops, so I think evolution in the future will involve functionality and versatility. Pretty soon phones should be able to sense a finger near but not touching the screen, allowing for hover states on mobile. I also think instead of having a desktop or laptop at home; cell phones will become your one, and only workhorse and people will just connect it to different interfaces and then back up their files to the cloud."

**Mitchell Barker** suggests that "if you look at where voice, in general, is going, we are moving towards Voice over IP systems, where clients no longer need to be registered with cellphone providers to make and receive calls – think Skype, WhatsApp, etc. It is an interesting concept to think that perhaps we are moving away from Telephone numbers altogether – where our email or personal ID is our telephone number. In that case, the device will use many mechanisms to connect with other subscribers – that could be ubiquitous Public Wi-Fi, Data only SIMS or local Wireless connection points. I don't foresee too much happening with devices for the next few years, other than some of this functionality will be integrated into wearable devices – some of which will work in conjunction with the mobile device, or completely independent."

**Mike McRitchie** says, "Currently smartphones have incorporated the phone, calendar, calculator, camera, camcorder, map, email, the internet, and many computer functions. It is amazing how many things used to be separate devices that are now on a smartphone in the palm of your hand. Convenience and instant answers are what make it so addicting. And addicting it is.

"I've also seen the development of the iPad, Apple Watch, and Fit Bit that is taking over more and more of the cell phone's functions for specific uses when people want a different aspect emphasized, (like a bigger screen with a tablet or a smaller, more portable device with the watch or fitness device).

"I don't think that the cell phone is going away, but I do see the phone being less important as people shy away from making "phone calls" and relying more on other forms of messaging. And, I do see that there will continue to be a push towards wifi connections, and small cell solutions in the wireless infrastructure side so that your use of the cell phone is more seamless.

"Where I see the cell phone, as we see it today, disappear is when there is a small device that can project the information onto a virtual screen - rather than having to carry that screen with you. That is where the true opportunity lies."

**Darius Allen** says, "The future of smartphones is in extended battery life. The phones of the future will be able to retain power for days or weeks at a time without a charge. That's just the tip of the iceberg; An unbreakable screen is something that we are actively pursuing."

**Jack Lombard** says, "I wouldn't be surprised if one day we searched the web by the power of our brainwaves. With Facebook developing A. I. from the data they're collecting from its users, that thought isn't so farfetched. Just Google search A.I. Development. **The writing is on the wall.**

# The Internet of Things

**S**amsung's website gives the best definition I've seen of the IoT, short for Internet of Things. They explain it as "shorthand for the way gadgets talk to each other."

Boiled down to its essentials, the Internet of Things is an amalgamation of switches and sensors connected by cellular technology. When a switch is activated, or a sensor tripped, it sends a signal to a connected device to do something.

Eventually, just about everything will be connected. Did you go to the grocery store without your shopping list? No problem. Pull up your smartphone APP, and check your refrigerator's contents. Are you almost out of toilet paper? An APP will alert you to bring another roll on your next trip to the restroom. Don't want to get up to restart the dryer, with a smart dryer you can do it from your smartphone APP. And, have you ever had that nagging feeling when you left home that you forgot to lock the doors or close the windows? Don't worry. Your APP will lock the door, and let you know which windows, if any, were left open.

The Internet of Things offers unlimited possibilities, but at the same time, it presents infinite dangers.

Author Robert Siciliano, suggests the IoT will "make dumb objects smarter. Imagine house keys that don't need to be taken out of one's purse or pocket to open a door or a gadget that can scan dairy products in your refrigerator for expiration dates, and the sensor will then remind you of these dates." There will be other *things* that "make changes by sensing changes in the environment. Imagine a garage door that opens because a sensor in it *knows* that the homeowner is approaching from 100 feet away."

But, he also foresees problems. "Imagine what a hacker can do: The whole town's garage doors won't open." Or, "imagine a *thing* sensing a change in your body (via sensory technology and APPs), and then responding by dispensing medication. But this also sounds frightening: Imagine what a malicious hacker can do with this technology."

**We live in dangerous times**, but it's also a time of amazing possibilities.

Whether we're ready for it, or not, the Internet of Things is going to change our lives similar to the way automobiles, airplanes, computers, telephones, and smartphones did. The biggest difference is the Internet of Things isn't going to be any one "thing." It's going to come in a million different sizes, shapes, and textures. It could be your dog's collar, a child's toy, an automobile tire, or even your favorite recliner.

The Internet of Things is about unlimited possibilities. If someone can think it, someone will create a "thing" to make it happen.

**Author's Note**: I go into detail about a large number of individual products in this section. The reason is the Internet of Things is no one individual thing. In the future, just about everything will be connected. The Internet of Things is more specific and product focused than anything we've seen so far. I just want to assure you there are no affiliate links in this section, or anywhere in this book. When I talk about a specific product, it is solely to let you know what's out there, or what I think may be coming down the pipeline.

# Drones

**Right now, everything you hear** about drones focuses on their use as an unmanned package delivery service for Amazon. But, that's just where the media is concentrated. As soon as drones go mainstream, they're going to revolutionize any number of services.

*Imagine your annual camping trip to Wildcat Den State Park. Everyone is packing up their stuff, getting ready to head back to base camp, after a day-long hike to the Devil's Punch Bowl. That's when you notice, your five-year-old daughter, Tori—has gone missing.*

*She helped gather firewood at lunch, and mom remembers her rolling around in the snow before lunch. After that, everyone draws a blank.*

*You begin a hurried search through the nearby woods. Everyone fans out, hollering "Tori!" and pokes around in the tall grass and bushes, but no Tori.*

*You call the park ranger. He understands your concern, but it's going to take him several hours to mount a search party. He's got to call in a helicopter and mobilize a ground crew to begin the search. In the meantime, all you can do is wait—and hope.*

*It's going to start getting dark in less than two hours, and the temperature has already dropped below freezing. Overnight temperatures are supposed to drop well below zero with wind chills. That doesn't give you much time.*

*Under normal circumstances, the search would be called off after dark, and everyone would be ready to hit the ground first thing in the morning. That leaves your daughter—lost, frightened, and alone in the woods overnight.*

*Now picture the same situation with a half-dozen drones buzzing over the park. They can check in nooks and crannies that would take normal searchers hours to reach. Because the drones are armed with infrared cameras, darkness is no barrier. Drones can fly day and night, with only occasional return visits to switch battery packs.*

*Skilled drone pilots could crisscross a five-mile grid around your campsite until they find your daughter. And, once they locate her, they could hover overhead, to help searchers pinpoint her location.*

**The hours after a storm hits** are often more deadly than the storm itself.

In most cases, roads get blocked by fallen trees and other debris. It could take days, even weeks for rescue crews to cut and dig their way through the carnage. Depending on how remote the affected area is, it could take a day or more to bring in a helicopter, and drop much needed medical supplies.

A squadron of drones doesn't face any similar barriers. Crews can load supplies into the drone's storage area and have them airborne within minutes. Hypothetically, in a remote area, like rural Montana, rescuers could send wave after wave of drones carrying medicines, water, and other needed supplies.

As they make their mercy run, the drones could record video footage of storm damage, road conditions, etc. In cases where remote localities are cut off with no other form of communication, messages could be sent back and forth by drone (similar to how carrier pigeons delivered messages in the past).

**Drones may eventually help** us predict the weather more accurately.

In the movie *Twister*, a crew of research scientists risked their lives to drive storm sensing equipment into a tornado so they could get a better understanding of what happens inside the eye of a tornado. Drone research is attempting to do the same thing; only it takes humans out of the danger zone.

*CO. EXIST*[47] reports Warren Causey, and his crew at Sirens Project,[48] are developing drones they can fly into tornadoes to collect more data. Their plan is to have the drone enter the edge of a tornado at speeds approaching 100 mph. At that point, their craft will be sucked into the vortex, and hop a ride on its air currents, recording data as it moves through the storm. One of their hopes is that they can collect enough data to help home builders erect stronger homes that can better resist storms.

Oklahoma researchers are developing drones that can withstand tornadic strength winds, in the hope they can gather more accurate data on temperature, humidity, and pressure. The information would provide another crucial link to enable them to predict storms more accurately. At the very least, they would like to collect more accurate information that could help them predict when and where twisters are likely to form.

The National Oceanic and Atmospheric Administration (NOAA) maintains a fleet of unmanned vehicles, codenamed *Coyote Drones*. These are small flyers, usually less than three feet long, that weigh under fifteen pounds, and have a wingspan that approaches six feet.

---

[47] Peters, Adele. *These Drones Will Fly Directly into Tornadoes to Predict Future Storms*. CO. EXIST. October 30, 2014.
[48] Sirens Project. Web. http://www.thesirensproject.com/

The *Coyote Drones* are normally launched from the belly of an airplane and controlled by pilots located in nearby planes. In 2014, the NOAA launched four drones into the eye of Hurricane Edouard. By doing this, they were better able to record the storm's continuous pressure, temperature, wind, and humidity. Getting a better handle on this information will help the NOAA more accurately forecast and predict storms.

**I'm a food delivery person's worst** nightmare. Most days, I'm more than happy to get lunch or supper myself, but storms bring out the wimp in me. About three years ago, we had a crazy-ass snow storm. Nearly two feet of whiteness fell in twenty-four hours, and nobody's car was going anywhere. Traffic had come to a complete standstill.

The snow plows worked like wild men as they tried to dig out the main drags. By late in the afternoon, they made one pass through my street. It was just enough for a car to squeeze through. That was all I needed to know. I was eating home delivery that night. I called Good2Go delivery services and placed my order—ribs, burgers, fries, and onion rings. They reminded me the weather was rough outside and said I should allow a little extra time for delivery.

I have to tell you; I was betting against that kid ever making it. The snow was still coming down. My sidewalk drifted over. And, *he didn't have a spot to pull into to make his delivery. Talk about having the deck stacked against you.*

To my surprise, the abominable delivery boy rang my doorbell an hour and twenty-three minutes later. He'd left his car running in the middle of the street, and sprinted through knee high snow drifts to get to the house. And, after all, that, he had a smile on his face. I still feel bad for only giving him a ten-dollar tip.

The problem is many restaurants, and delivery services pull their drivers off the roads on stormy nights because it's unsafe for them to be out. It makes sense. But, it costs the restaurant money and leaves customers with a bad taste in their mouth and an empty feeling in their belly.

What if restaurants could still deliver your food without the risk to their drivers or their vehicles? It would be a win-win for everyone.

Domino's Pizza in the UK has been experimenting with something called The DomiCopter. It's an octocopter style drone (it has eight propellers), built tough enough to hold several large pizzas.

I wouldn't have believed it if I hadn't seen the YouTube[49] video. It shows the DomiCopter in flight, carrying a blue Domino's

---

[49] *Introducing the Domino's DomiCopter!* Web. https://www.youtube.com/watch?v=on4DRTUvst0

delivery pack clutched in its claws. You see it buzzing across the country, over trees, over water, and right up to a homeowner waiting for his pizza. He unloads the Domino's bag, and heads to the house, as the drone makes its way back to the launch pad.

You're not likely to see a drone delivering your pizza anytime soon because current laws prohibit commercial usage of drones. The idea is intriguing, though. It could provide quicker delivery for pizza lovers, and save on fuel costs for restaurant operators. The real question is without a pizza delivery driver, who gets the tip?

# Wearables

**R**ight now, **wearables are seen** as more of an add-on for your smartphone, rather than a standalone product. There's a good chance that will change going forward. "As devices integrate into our daily lives and workflow," says Austin Smith, "wearables will make it easier and easier to stay in sync across all our devices - and that means that eventually, smartphones will be obsolete."

A study by Gartner,[50] reports **wearable** sales are expected to jump to eighteen percent in 2016

Bluetooth headsets, those clip-on devices that allow you to talk hands-free, are by far the best selling wearable. Sales will reach close to 130 million units worldwide in 2016. Sales of smartwatches are expected to reach 50 million units this year, up from 30 million in 2015.

---

[50] *Gartner Says Worldwide Wearable Devices Sales to Grow 18.4 Percent in 2016.* Gartner. February 2, 2016.

**Here's the funny thing.** As smartphone screens are getting larger, manufacturers are racing to see who can develop a smaller screened device. They're all competing to develop the "breakthrough" smartwatch.

Back in the mid-1970's calculator watches were the height of high tech. Microsoft released the first computerized watch in 1982. Seiko developed the first internet-connected watch in 1984. They called it the Wrist Terminal. To connect to another computer or the internet required a proprietary cable.

Smartwatches have come a long way since then. There are dozens of models available, but three brands currently dominate the market Apple, Samsung, and Pebble.

Like so many other things in high tech, compatibility is the first issue smartwatch buyers need to tackle. Your choices are Apple IOS or Android. Currently, no one makes a smartwatch compatible with Blackberry or Windows phones. If you're undecided or looking for a smartwatch that goes, either way, the Pebble is a good choice. It lets you connect to Apple, or Android smartphones, using your Bluetooth connection.

If you're still on the line about which smartwatch is right for you, check out its APPs store. Does it offer smartwatch based versions of the APPs you use most? The "Apple watch only (officially) works with iPhones and iPads," says Jaq Andrews, "and Android wear watches only (officially) work with Android devices.

If you want fancy APPs on your phone, choose the one that matches the phone you're already invested in." Keep in mind, right now APP developers favor Apple IOS, Pebble, then Android. That means you have your best chance of finding your favorite APP on an Apple watch.

If you are trying to decide between a smartwatch and a fitness tracker, let me warn you up front, no smartwatch is really up to the task. Most smartwatches count footsteps, a few monitor your heartbeat, but that's where it ends. Smartwatches don't provide all the reports and extras that fitness trackers do. "Fitness tracking is one function of most smartwatches," says Jaq Andrews. "Dedicated fitness trackers are usually cheaper and a bit more rugged, but can't download and install new APPs. Some fitness trackers can interact with a very limited number of APPs on your phone, like notifying you of text messages, but many don't even have screens – all they do is record your movements via an accelerometer and sync that data with a smartphone APP over Bluetooth."

When you're wearing a smartwatch, you have a miniature version of your smartphone on your wrist. It can run APPs, play videos, and stream music to a Bluetooth headset. Another great feature is you can sync it with your smartphone. Once you do this, you can send text messages, receive notifications from your email and social media accounts, and make and receive phone calls.

Joggers, and exercise enthusiasts, like smartwatches because they can leave their bulky phones at home or in their lockers, and still have access to everything while they are working out. Students enjoy the fact it's compact and easily kept out of sight. Smartwatches make it easy for them to keep up with texts and social media notifications while they are in class. And, when class lets out, they can clip on their Bluetooth headset to catch up on missed calls.

"I am surprised at how much I use it," says Anne Louise Bannon, a writer, and columnist, "especially for fitness tracking, but also keeping on top of things while working out. I got a work email not too long ago and was able to jump on it, rather than wait to get my phone out. That being said, smart watches are still a solution in search of a problem. An insanely cool solution, but still in search of a real problem."

A recent study conducted by MBLM,[51] a brand intimacy agency, discovered "over the past six months, the Apple watch is being used less and less as its novelty wears off." One thing MBLM determined over the course of their six-month study is users went from "love to like." Users "continue to like the watch. A few are happy with it, while most have lost the love feeling." One of the main complaints users have about the Apple watch is "many

---

[51] *Apple Watch Study: Part 3. The Six Month Itch. Is the Thrill Gone.* MBLM. Web. http://mblm.com/apple-watch/apple-watch-study-part-3-the-six-month-itch

functions available on the watch are more complicated to access than those on the phone." One result is, they go back to their iPhone to complete the task.

One reason MBLM gives for users ditching their Apple watches is the marketplace hasn't caught up with everything the watch has to offer. "The lag with retail, travel and hospitality companies accommodating the watch for payment, access or other wallet features has continued to negatively impact its penetration and popularity." What that suggests is the watch may become more popular as more retailers accept payments through the device, and as more "useful" APPs become available.

It may be the smartwatch is still ahead of its time.

Two of the biggest disadvantages of using a smartwatch are the small screen size and limited battery life. The big challenge for developers and users is viewing everything on one inch or one and one-half inch screens. It forces you to minimize everything. Battery life is another sore spot. Smartwatches suck up a lot of juice. Just figure, your smartwatch is going to need to hit the charger every night, the same as your smartphone. Jaq Andrews sums it up this way. "A watch needs to be instantly available but low power, which is still a challenge. If anyone perfects a constant information display that doesn't deplete the battery, that company will sell a lot of smartwatches."

The only way around that right now is to choose a device like the Pebble. "Pebble is interesting because it syncs with both Apple and Android devices," says Jaq Andrews, "but doesn't have the real backing of either. Pebble watches don't have the brilliant displays of other smartwatches, but their batteries last a lot longer, so they appeal to people who want a watch with some extra features."

One final consideration is aesthetics. While smartwatches are small, they still look big and bulky on your wrist. A recent article in *Racked*[52] magazine suggests smartwatches are unpopular with women for this very reason. They back that up with data from a *Consumers and Wearables*[53] report from NPD Connected Intelligence. It said one in ten American adults own a fitness tracker, and the usage is split pretty much evenly between men and women. With smartwatches, 71 percent of the people who own them are male. They don't see the market (for women) picking up until smartwatches get thinner and more stylish.

**If you're looking for something** more basic, you can get a fitness tracker like the Fitbit for as little as $99. Compare that to

---

[52] Fumo, Nicola. *Why Women Aren't Buying Smartwatches.* Racked Magazine. January 12, 2016.
[53] *Wear Report. Industry Overview and Forecast.* NPD Connected Intelligence. April 2015.

smartwatches that retail for anywhere between $199 and $599 (for the high-end Apple watch).

The difference is a fitness tracker like the Fitbit collects data you can track on your computer or smartphone APP. Basic information tracked by the Fitbit includes steps taken, distance traveled, calories burned, and sleep time and quality. It also has a vibrating alarm to wake you up gently.

The FitBit Flex lets you set fitness goals. During your workout, you tap the wristband twice to see how close you are to reaching your goal. When you reach your goal, the FitBit lights up and vibrates to let you know you did it. After your workout, you can track your goals on the smartphone APP, and keep a progress log.

The problem is fitness tracking devices aren't all they're cracked up to be. Users are psyched up when they get them, but for many, the relationship sours quickly.

A recent article in the *Journal of the American Medical Association*[54] says only fifty percent of people who purchase a fitness tracking device continue to use it over the long haul. Roughly one-third of purchasers give up using the device within six months. Some of that is likely due to the fact counting steps sucks all the fun out of exercise because of the relentless push to take more steps. At least that's the reason many users give when

---

[54] Patel, Mitesh H. *Wearable Devices as Facilitators, Not Drivers, of Health Behavior Changes*. JAMA. The Journal of the American Medical Association. February 3, 2015.

asked why they scrapped their FitBits and other fitness tracking devices. It's too much like having your high school gym teacher come along for the ride—reminding you how to move properly, and screaming that "you're a quitter" if you don't take one more step.

**Got a new baby? There's a gadget** to help with just about anything you need to do for her. Take her temperature remotely, monitor her movements, check up on her sleep patterns, and diagnose illnesses over the phone.

Here are a few recent innovations to give you an idea where the baby wearables market is headed.

Installing the *MonBaby* monitor is about as easy as it gets. It's a button you attach to your baby's onesie. After you hook it up, it lets you monitor her sleep position (back or stomach), breathing movements, and it sends an alert if it senses she has fallen. Just attach the button, pull up the smartphone APP, and you can monitor your baby's sleep time from the comfort of your living room. It will also send you an alert if your baby changes its sleep position or rolls from its back to its stomach. It's a quick, easy way to stop worrying about Sudden Infant Death Syndrome (SIDS).

*One of the worst fears any parent has is leaving young children when they're sick. Most likely, it's just a cold, or fever, and nothing to worry about. But, what if. You understand. Just before my* youngest daughter turned one, she had an ear infection and started running a fever. Several hours later, she was sleeping in my arms when I noticed her eyes roll back into her head. Talk about a heart-stopping moment!

My fingers dialed 9-1-1. In no time, I had a house full of firemen, policemen, and paramedics. Our whole world was turned upside down because of an ear infection. The way the doctors explained it, her fever spiked and caused her to go into seizures. Everything turned out okay that time. But a couple of months later the same thing happened again when my wife was holding her. By the time doctors got her breathing on her own again they a had a helicopter on the pad waiting to fly her to University Hospitals.

We were lucky both times, but talk about panic any time after that when she had a fever.

That was in 2001. Medical wearables were a futuristic dream then. So were smartphones and APPs. Today, there's a gadget that could have made things a whole lot easier on us. TempTraq created a smart thermometer strip. You just attach the strip under your baby's arms, and it remains active for 24 hours. Once you have the patch attached, you can monitor your baby's temperature from the smartphone APP. You can program it to send alerts if her temperature reaches a specified level. That would have made things a whole lot easier on us then.

*Sproutling* bills itself as the "world's first sensing, learning, predicting baby monitor."

What does that mean?

It's a smart band that straps around your baby's ankle. It senses your child's temperature, motion, and position. Parents can monitor everything from *Sproutling's* smartphone APP. But, as they say, it's not about the numbers. *Sproutling* learns about your baby as it monitors her activities. If you've got a party, or event coming up, it can help you predict how long she will sleep. It also sends out alerts, so you know immediately if your baby is running a fever or changes its sleeping position.

*iSwimband* makes a device parents have wished for, for several generations. It comes as a headband for swimmers, and a wristband for non-swimmers. Once your child is wearing it, you can monitor their movements on a smartphone APP. The swimmer version alerts you if it senses your child is under water for longer than the pre-set period you specify. The non-swimmer version alerts you if your child falls into a body of water. Another device, the *SunFriend*, warns users if they are in danger of being sunburned. That way they can get out of the sun, or apply more sun blocker before any serious skin damage can occur.

These are just a few of the wearables being developed to monitor babies and younger children. In time, I would expect to see less expensive devices that go with your child, day and night, and perform multiple functions. As time goes by, devices that solve just one problem will most likely fall by the wayside.

**Got a pet, the IoT has a "thing"** to help you keep track of him. If there's one thing people like as much as their kids, it's their pets. If you have any doubts, look at all those kitty videos crowding out your *Facebook Timeline*.

In the dog world, one of the newest wearables to hit the market is the *Connected Collar*. The latest one is called *Buddy*, and reviews on its Indiegogo[55] crowdfunding page suggest it's "the Apple Watch of dog collars" [*Mashable*], and "a FitBit for your dog" [*The Independent*].

*Buddy* monitors your pet's daily activities through a built-in GPS system so that you can track its whereabouts in real time. Whether you're looking for your dog in the house, or outside, you can find him quickly using your smartphone APP. The collar's LED lighting is bright and ensures your pet gets noticed by cars, pedestrians, and bikers. That means there's less chance your pet will be involved in an accident if he gets loose.

*Buddy's* smartphone APP provides an overview of what's going on with your pet. A quick glance displays temperature, activity, social alerts, and a calendar of events. If your dog likes to wander,

---

[55] *Buddy. The Dog Collar Reimagined.* Indiegogo. Web. https://www.indiegogo.com/projects/buddy-the-dog-collar-re-imagined#/

you can set up a geofence around your home. Buddy will send you alerts if he strays outside of the preset boundaries. If you're worried about your pet's fitness, you can track his steps, sleep time, and calories burned. The social community feature of the APP lets you know where your friends are and allows you to comment on their routines or share your dog's stats.

The manufacturer bills *FitBark* as the *FitBit* for your dog. The company says your dog is the "ideal workout partner." Their "mission is to get dogs and humans healthy together." The device monitors your dog's day-to-day activities and gives you reports on his sleep patterns, movements, etc.

It tracks your dog's activities, shows how far he walked during the day, how long he slept, and when he slept. The built-in GPS lets you keep track of your dog's whereabouts at any given time.

Another similar device is the *Tagg* pet tracking system. The *Tagg* lets you track your pet's activity and location. If your pet goes lost, you can track him in the mobile APP, or if you text "LOCATE" to 52366, *Tagg* will text your dog's current location to you. It also has an ambient temperature sensor so you can tell if your pet is hot or cold.

Keep a close eye on the pet wearables market, because it's poised to explode. People love their pets. They will spend whatever it takes to keep them safe and happy. I can't tell you what it's going to be, but I bet you pet clothes are going to be hot—jackets, headbands, booties, etc. And, they won't just track your pet's location. Expect them to monitor your pet's vitals and temperature. My guess is there will be some sort of front-facing camera, so you can monitor what kind of mischief your little "angel" is engaging in. And, it wouldn't surprise me a bit if there was a microphone and speaker so you could talk to and listen to your pet.

# Medical Innovations

**Wearables are finding a solid home** in the medical field. Caregivers use them to monitor temperatures, diagnose illnesses, and track Alzheimer's and dementia patients.

Bruce Barnet, from Healthcare Products, LLC says, "Wearable technologies [for the medical field] come in all different forms, but the hottest market is the GPS tracker for the elderly. This is specific for caregivers needing to track those with Alzheimer's, dementia, autism and memory loss."

He says, "the term *tracker* is generally used when describing a GPS locator device, but the more precise way to describe it is as a *wandering device*, and there is a difference. A difference that can mean life or death." Tracking devices come in a variety of shapes and sizes, but to be a *true wandering prevention device for the elderly* it needs to be "secured to the body, and this only comes in a watch with a lockable wristband." Another technology, *Smart*

*Soles*, are shoe pads that fit in a patient's shoes. The problem with that is "people that wander have a tendency to shed their clothes" so the technology is not 100 percent effective.

GPS locators are good around the house, where memory patients have easy access to doors. If the person goes missing, caregivers can track them via a smartphone APP or tablet. "Now we are finding that facilities are buying them," says Barnet. "Although all memory care facilities are locked down units, patients do find ways to wander off, or just find places to hide within the facility. With the *Freedom Watch* and a battery that lasts up to 30 days, any nurse can see from her nursing station exactly where their patient is all the time."

One problem Barnet sees with GPS locator devices is they "usually tell you where the wearer is when you go looking for them, but it does not alert you when they have gone *wandering*. Many times that is too late to save their life. In general, there is a fifteen-minute delay between the signal and monitoring location, so when you find them with a tracker, they can be gone or drowned.

"A wandering device like *Freedom Watch* by *Lok8u* or *Iloc* alerts you **immediately** should the wearer leave a preset area (a GEO fence). Their location can be seen precisely, in real time, on a tablet computer, or smartphone. The device sends out an alert to three designated recipients so [the patient] can be located and found immediately. Hopefully, before they get out of the local area. It can even tell you if the person has left the GEO fence between the house and a pool if it is set to do that."

That's a win-win for patients and caregivers and gives a better chance for finding *wandering* patients before they come to harm.

Barnet sees several changes coming down the pipeline for wearable medical devices. "New technologies will incorporate many of the features that we find in the Fit Bit, and other medical devices including medication reminders, 24/7 emergency alerts, fall detection, and step gait analysis.

"Patient shoes will have a toe plate, and when it comes in contact with their door, it will unlock." Personally, he thinks, "the cell phone giants, like AT&T and Verizon, will take over this industry where monitoring is involved. They have the retail outlets, and it seems a natural fit."

**One of the bigger problem** faced by doctors is how to get patients to take their medications. They can prescribe the correct medicines to control high blood pressure and regulate your heartbeat, but once a patient leaves his office, it's up to them to take their medicines.

A company named Vitality created an easy to use solution to remind users it's time to take your meds. GlowCaps replace the regular lids on your prescription bottles. The cap lights up if the user is more than 30 minutes late taking their medicine. After an hour and a half, the cap lights up and emits an alert. If the user is over two hours late taking their medicine, the GlowCap system sends them a text message or telephones them.

If GlowCaps stopped right there, they'd be a great reminder system. What's unique, is they can send a weekly alert to physicians or loved ones to let them know whether you're taking your medicines or not. There's also a button you can press on the cap to order a refill. When you press the button, it dials your pharmacy.

**Falls present a real danger** to elderly and disabled individuals. One slip can cause them to lose their independence. Studies show, one in three adults over age 65 falls each year. When an elderly individual falls, they risk hip and head injuries. If they live alone, there is an increased risk of death because there is no one available to assist them.

The reality is the longer a fall victim goes undetected; the more likely the person is to sustain a serious injury that will require long-term care.

For seniors, a single fall can result in the loss of independence. Sometimes they can move in with a family member, but often, injuries related to a fall mean an extended stay in an assisted living facility, or that they have to move to a nursing home. Fall detectors can't prevent falls, but they can lead to early detection which can increase the odds of shorter recovery times.

Fall detectors can sense your movements and the position of your body. They can determine the difference between when you're laying down sleeping, or if you're body has made a directional shift and fallen-down. The devices also monitor your movements, thirty seconds before, and after it detects a fall. If it doesn't sense any movement within thirty seconds after it senses a fall, the device sends out an alert.

**Right now, pacemakers** and cardiac defibrillators can automatically transmit data to healthcare providers. Over the next few years, doctors will be able to implant sensors that notify them when the patient is at risk of a cardiac event. Imagine your doctor being able to call you to warn you that you need to seek treatment immediately. It will be possible to implant a sensor under a diabetic patient's skin that can monitor their blood sugar levels and skin temperatures and automatically trigger an insulin pump to deliver the correct dosage of medicine.

Eventually, the healthcare paradigm is going to shift. Instead of you calling the doctor when you feel sick or a little off, the doctor is going to call you. Your toilet is going to monitor your urine and "poo." Implants are going to monitor your heart rate, blood pressure, insulin, and sugar levels. Your doctor will receive alerts when something goes off kilter, and he can tweak your medicines, schedule additional tests, or warn you—something "big" is about to happen, and you need to get to the hospital now.

# Connected House

*One of the most visited exhibitions* at the 1933 Chicago World's Fair was the **Homes of Tomorrow**. The display consisted of twelve model homes, but the one that knocked everyone's socks off was **The House of the Future** designed by Chicago architect George Frederick Keck. It was a three-story, circular building with glass windows all around it.

The lower level featured a two-car garage—one for your car, and another for your airplane (futurists assumed airplanes would be as common as cars in the not so distant future). None of the windows were functional. No one saw a need for them. Keck envisioned a home where a built in central air conditioning system would control the temperature.

The kitchen was a housewife's dream. It came loaded up with modern appliances—an "iceless" electric refrigerator, a modern stove, and a mechanical dishwasher that washed and dried dishes. The kitchen door was connected to a light sensor. When *the beam was broken, it triggered the door to open and close automatically. And, for entertainment, the house featured a new and untested piece of technology soon to be ensconced in every home—a television set.*

While the model homes were extremely popular, most exhibition guests said they wouldn't want to live in them. They described the houses as "cold," "strange," and "not homelike."

The *Connected House*, like the *House of the Future*, may appear "strange" and "cold" at first if we are not careful. We also need to be careful not to overlook unseen opportunities. Keck built *The House of the Future* during the Chicago winter where temperatures can quickly fall well below zero. One day, he noticed his workers had stripped off their jackets when they were working inside of the unheated house. When asked why, they said they were warm, even though it was a blustery, cold day outside. That got Keck to thinking about solar energy. He tucked that information away in the vault, and when he came back to it later, he became a champion of solar homes throughout the 1940s and 1950s.

Because of this, it's important that we carefully evaluate new bits of technology before we discard them. What appears unimportant, or inconsequential, at the time, may later prove to be a game changer.

**There's nothing new about** the *Connected House*. We've had devices and timers available for several decades that let you turn lights on and off, or switch the coffee pot on at the same time your alarm goes off. How many of you remember the *CLAPPER*? "Clap on. Clap off." And, the light turns off / on—sometimes. The *Connected House* works on the same principle, the only difference is, it can connect and control, a multitude of devices—not just one.

Right now, many of us already have smart devices in our homes—programmable thermostats, digital security systems, etc. But, that's just the tip of the iceberg. The *Connected House* is going to become one with you. It's going to learn your habits, your movements, your likes, and dislikes. It's going to know what you like to watch on TV, the kind of music you like to listen to, and which video games you play incessantly. It will anticipate your needs and offer you smart choices.

The idea behind the *Connected House* is to provide a safer, more comfortable home. It will automatically control the interior temperatures and turn lights on and off as you leave the room. A sophisticated digital security system will enable the house to protect itself with a combination of smoke detectors, carbon monoxide detectors, door and window sensors, and high definition cameras.

Homeowners will be able to check up on, and monitor, all aspects of their homes directly from their smartphone.

"I'm particularly impressed with Samsung SmartThings," says Dave Johnson of Techwalla, a consumer tech product review site. "They made a great move by buying SmartThings—they got a great, innovative product that's at the bleeding edge of the IoT, and they can now leverage that with their substantial corporate muscle. To be honest, I really haven't seen them do that yet— Samsung is being really timid right now on the smart home front—but I think in the medium term, they have a great shot at becoming the industry leader for a smart home platform that the rest of the industry aligns itself around."

**SmartThings is a popular solution** for people who want to automate their homes on the cheap. In this section, I'm going to give an overview of *SmartThings*, and then I'm going to examine some one-off devices you can get started with today, so you can test-drive living in a smart home.

Samsung's *SmartThings* is a quick and easy way to automate your home—with little, or no installation required. The main component of the system is the *SmartThings* Hub. It connects wirelessly with the *SmartThings* sensors and devices you install in your home. After you have your Hub set up, you can monitor everything from your smartphone APP. The APP lets you set up alerts, so you know when certain things happen, such as a water leak, or if someone enters or leaves the house. You can set it up to trigger certain actions automatically, such as to turn on the coffee pot in the morning, or to turn off the TV or stereo at a predetermined time.

Some of the components that make up *SmartThings* include a motion sensor, a multi-sensor, a smart power outlet, a presence sensor, and a moisture monitor.

The motion sensor helps you keep track of unwanted, or unexpected, goings on in your home while you are away. Motion sensors can be used to trigger a light to turn on as you enter another room. The multi-sensor monitors doors, windows, garages, and cabinets to let you know whether they are open or closed. You no longer need to wonder whether you left the windows open during a storm—your phone will tell you. The *Smart Power* Outlet is the key to controlling connected lights, electronics, and other small appliances. You can program them to turn off and on automatically, or you can hop on the APP, and control them at will.

If you constantly find yourself searching for lost keys or other objects, you're going to love the presence sensor. It functions as a quick finding device. You can clip one to a child's jacket, or jeans, and it will alert you when they enter or leave the house. Attach it to a pet's collar, and you will know if they are in the house, or outside. If you habitually misplace your keys, the sensor can be set to emit a beep, so your keychain is easier to find. The moisture sensor can be placed in basements, attics, or bathrooms to help you discover leaks before they become major problems.

**Crazy as it sounds, *Amazon Echo*** probably has the best chance at delivering on the promise of the truly connected house.

Essentially, *Amazon Echo* is a speaker with a twist. I'm not sure the folks at Amazon even know what they have. They release new updates frequently to add to its repertoire.

The gadget itself is a small, black, circular object that stands 9.25 inches tall, and 3.27 inches around. It's got a 2" tweeter, a 2.5-inch woofer, and an array of 7 microphones at the top to power its voice recognition software. Like Apple and "Siri," Echo has a persona named "Alexa." If you want it to do something, you say "Alexa, (followed by your command)."

Obviously, you can use it to listen to music. It connects with Amazon related services such as Amazon Prime Music, Spotify, Pandora, IHeartRadio, TuneIn, and Amazon Music. If you have an iPhone or iPad, you can pair it with *Echo* over Bluetooth, and use it as a wireless speaker.

One of the smartest moves Amazon made was to allow *Echo* to connect with other devices easily. If you use lights and switches from WeMo, Phillips Hue, Samsung Smart Things, Insteon, or Wink, you can use *Echo* to control your devices. Just say, "Alexa, dim my bedroom lights." "Alexa, turn on the TV." "Alexa, turn on my fan." Alexa will listen to what you say and do it. It's a whole lot easier and quicker than pulling up one of the other guy's smartphone APPs because you can just say what you want *Echo* to do.

*Echo* also offers a great way to stay up to date on news, weather, and the stock market. Just say, "Alexa, what is the news?" "Alexa, what is the weather?" or "Alexa, what is the stock market news?" If you listen to audio books, *Echo* integrates smoothly with Audible to play your books. Just say, "Alexa, play the book [title]." Alexa can also read select *Kindle Unlimited* books using the text to speech feature.

And, speaking of the text to speech feature, you can use it to read *Wikipedia* articles. Just remember, you need to precede any request with the word *Wikipedia*, so to listen to an article on the Black Hawk War, you would say, "*Wikipedia*: Black Hawk War."

Have you ever created a shopping list, pulled it up at the store, and got home to discover you missed something or maybe had someone ask— "Why didn't you get----?" *Echo* lets everybody add to your list while you are out and about. That way, when you pull it up at the store, it's fresh and up to date.

*TechCrunch*[56] says, Domino's Pizza now lets you order pizza using the *Amazon Echo*. To get started, users first need to set up a *Pizza Profile* with Domino's (basically your ordering information, name, address, and payment method). After your profile is set up,

---

[56] Perez, Sarah. *Amazon Echo Can Now Order Your Pizza.* Tech Crunch. February 3, 2016

you need to say, "Alexa, open Domino's and place my Easy Order." *Echo* users also need to take one additional step before placing their first order. They need to enable the Domino's skill in the Alexa APP and link it to their *Pizza Profile*.

*Echo* isn't the perfect solution for the *Connected House*, but it brings you closer than any other alternative available today.

Apple has recently joined the fray. IOS 10 comes equipped with a *HOME* APP to help users automate their home. It allows users to connect with devices from just about any manufacturer—SmartThings, Phillips Hue, WeMo, etc.

To get started, you just select "Add Device" and follow the prompts. Time will tell if it catches on. The biggest advantage Apple HOME has going for it is it ships pre-loaded on millions of new iPhones.

**Okay, I get it.** Like most of us, you live in a dumb house. You know when the tub overflows because your foot splashes in a puddle of water in the hallway or the upstairs bathroom floor comes crashing through the bedroom ceiling. A *Connected House* isn't in your future anytime soon. No worry. Here are a few ideas on how you can make your home smarter, one component at a time.

We've all heard about smart cars, smart houses, smart food, smart water, smart whatever, so I guess it was only a matter of time before someone created the smart toilet.

It used to be you'd just sit down, get your business done, flush, and walk away, but smart toilets are taking number one, and number two, to a whole new level. And, that begs the question—"What's going on with my poo?"

Panasonic began marketing their smart toilet in Japan in 1999. When you sit down, it calculates your weight, percent of body fat, and Body Mass Index (BMI). It also analyzes your urine and "poo," and can forward the results to a health monitoring service, or you can view details using an APP on your smartphone or tablet.

Another smart toilet taking Japan by the seat of the pants is the *Toto Intelligence Toilet II*. It has all the bells and whistles you'd expect from a luxury toilet. It analyzes your bodily excrements—BMI, blood sugar levels, and captures your body weight. It sports a heated seat, bidet, and air dryer. Connected options let you beam your health-related info directly to your doctor, or to an APP so you can check out all the details on your smartphone. At $6100, it's one of the more expensive components of the *Connected House*.

Koehler is marketing the *Numi* Smart Toilet in the United States. It features auto flush technology, with six flush cycles to save water. It has a self-cleaning bidet with an air dryer, adjustable water temperature, a heated seat, and foot warmer. It has a motion sensor to raise and lower the seat automatically, and it offers ambient lighting and stereo speakers with a built-in FM radio tuner. And, it comes with a remote control for easy programming. The price tag is a hefty $6400.

If you have trouble sleeping through the night *beddit* has created a sleep monitor to measure your sleep quality. It's non-invasive. Just slip the monitor under your bed sheets, and sleep on it. B*eddit's* literature says their monitor can turn any bed into a Smart Bed. *Beddit* analyzes your sleep and transmits the results to their APP. It rates your sleep quality on a scale of from 1 to 100, and a score in the "green zone" means you enjoyed a good night's sleep.

GE sells a full range of connected appliances branded under the name *GE Wifi Connect*. With their smartphone APP, you can stay connected to your stove, refrigerator, washer/dryer, and water heater from wherever you are.

If you own a GE smart refrigerator, it can send out alerts in case of a power outage, or send you a message that the door has been left open. It can also let you know when it's time to change the filter, or if the temperature is too high. You can turn the icemaker on or off, or program your refrigerator to have hot water ready for your morning coffee.

The washer/dryer APP lets users receive an alert when the cycle has finished. You can extend the dryer range (without getting up), and it lets users know how much time is left for the cycle to complete. You don't need to miss the most exciting moments of your TV shows to check if the washer or dryer cycle is done.

They also offer a *Geospring Hybrid* water heater that allows users to adjust the water temperature or set a vacation mode from their APP to save on energy costs. You can also receive maintenance alerts on your smartphone to ensure your device is running properly.

The *Nest* home thermostat adapts to your lifestyle and changes in the seasons. It learns your likes and dislikes and automatically makes those adjustments for you. If your lifestyle changes, the *Nest* thermostat changes with it. It continuously monitors your usage patterns and adapts to them. If for some reason your work schedule changes and you need to head home early, you can adjust the temperature of your home with the smartphone APP. That way your home can be as cool, or as warm, as you like. Another bonus is it lights up when you enter the room, and displays the temperature, so there's no guessing what temperature it's set at.

*Nest* also makes a unique smoke and $CO_2$ detector. What I like about it is you can turn it off from your smartphone, instead of tearing out the battery when the stove goes crazy and burns your latest edible creation. Another neat feature is a built-in motion sensor. When you walk under it, it shoots out a beam of light to help you find your way in the dark.

Here are a few connected devices for your furry friends.

*Pet Cube* lets you stay connected to your pet while you are on the go. It's sort of like a baby monitor for pets. The device has a 138° wide-angle camera that streams HD video. It features two-way voice streaming so that you can listen to your dog or talk to him. It's the next best thing to being with your pet. Just don't let the boss catch you talking to the dog on your smartphone. He could get the wrong idea.

For cat lovers, there's *Tailio*, the smart litter box. *Tailio* monitors your cat's weight, waste output, and frequency. It sends alerts to your smartphone if it spots unhealthy trends.

*PupPod* is an interactive toy for dogs. It consists of three parts. A *Kong* wobbler toy for your dog to play with, a *PupPod* hub that houses the video camera, and a feeder that dispenses treats as a reward. The *Kong* toy contains a motion sensor and communicates with the hub when it senses activity. Pet owners can watch live videos of their dog at play, trigger treat rewards, and record videos of their pets at play. The idea behind *PupPod* is an active dog is a healthy dog, and when you give a pet something to do, it is less likely to damage furniture or other items.

**No matter how you slice it**, the *Connected House* is still more fiction that fact.

"Smart home and IOT will remain the playground of hobbyists, tinkerers, and early adopters through this year," explains Dave Johnson. "There are simply a lack of compelling use cases. Take the very clever Flick buttons, for example. These are like a gateway drug to the IoT. But when you get down to the nitty-gritty, you find they only do a small handful of things, only one or two of which are practical for any particular real person. The reality of the immature state of smart home tech squashes that dream."

Do you remember Barney Stinson from *How I Met Your Mother*? He had a guy for everything. The smart house is currently in a similar state. Everybody has a solution. None of them work together, and none of them live up to the true promise of the *Connected House*. They automate certain tasks, but that's where it ends. You need a separate guy (device) to complete every task.

A *Connected House* is supposed to be an extension of the people who live in it. The *Connected House* is supposed to learn from its inhabitants and adapt to their lifestyles. After it does that, it should offer them smart choices that enhance their lifestyles. You shouldn't need a remote to program, and control, every function of your home life. All the components should work together seamlessly. Like the Nest thermostat, they should learn from what you do and automatically adjust to your preferences.

Until that happens, the *Connected House* is going to remain a dream.

The near future isn't going to be anything like the *Jetsons*. Your car isn't likely to fly anytime soon. It's unlikely we will have robot maids or live in houses that float in space. The odds are all that stuff is still a good hundred years off in the future. Maybe more.

# Connected Car

When most people think about the *Connected Car*, their minds turn to 4G LTE data, connected devices, and kick-ass sound systems, but the *Connected Car* is a whole lot more than that. Hidden within your car's operating system are hundreds of tiny interconnected sensors that work together to ensure your car runs at peak performance levels.

Right now, the sensors in your car check the air level in your tires, your coolant temperature, oil level, compression, and much, much more.

Tomorrow's *Connected Car* is going to have sensors built into your tires that gauge road temperature, and other dangerous road conditions, such as water, ice, and snow. When a possible threat is detected, your car will still display the *traction warning* light and *ice possible* warning to grab your attention. But, that's just the start of it. Tomorrow's *Connected Car* will sense threats, evaluate, and act on them instantaneously. If your car senses slippery pavement, it can adjust its onboard stability system, and send out a notification to other vehicles on the same road about potentially slippery conditions.

Tomorrow's *Connected Car* is going to have that kick-ass sound system you always wanted, but it's going to be driven by your smartphone. APPs and videos will display and function on your center console. Your phone already connects with most 2009 plus vehicles via Bluetooth. At the tap of a button, Siri will read your voice messages, or let you dictate messages. Android systems will display a limited number of Google Now cards that relate specifically to traveling.

Tomorrow's *Connected Car* is going to have the best onboard navigation system you've ever experienced. Unlike the previous manufacturer's systems, the new navigation systems are powered by Google Maps and Apple Maps. They will feature brighter, crisper displays. The turn-by-turn directions will be more detailed and accurate. And, they will make better suggestions about where to make a pit stop for gas, food, and lodging. More importantly, they will scan your route, and suggest alternate routes that will save you travel time, delays, and other headaches.

Tomorrow's car will be "connected." It will serve as a wireless hub to allow travelers to connect their devices. It will talk to other cars, and travel and weather beacons to pass on road conditions, travel delays, accident alerts, etc.

Automakers are hard at work developing semi-autonomous cars that can park themselves after the driver leaves the car. Google, Apple, and Tesla are racing each other to get the first fully autonomous vehicle to market.

Like the *Connected House*, the real purpose of the *Connected Car* is to provide users with a safer, more enjoyable driving experience. To make this possible, cars need to connect with other cars on the roads around them and provide an enhanced in-car experience. That means cars need onboard wireless internet so they can communicate back and forth with other vehicles. They also need a sophisticated system of sensors in the engine compartment, cabin, tires, and drive train. All the components need to work together, wirelessly, to keep the passengers safe and comfortable.

The problem for manufacturers is it will cost money to make those improvements, and while car buyers want, and demand smarter cars, they also say they're not willing to put up more money to pay for those features.

Something's got to give to make it all come together.

Truly *Connected Cars* are still a long way off. Infrastructure changes are necessary to make them work properly. Roadside sensors and in-road sensors are a must to communicate road conditions to vehicles. Cars are also going to need to communicate with each other to let oncoming traffic know about ice, snow, and other dangerous road conditions.

Today, less than eight percent of cars worldwide are connected. A report by *McKinsey*[57] says that number should jump to twenty-five percent by 2020. Most of the increase is expected to be in newer, higher-end vehicles.

*Business Insider* predicts that by 2020 seventy-five percent of cars on the road will have the equipment needed to connect to the internet, but only one-third of car owners will invest the time and money to hook up the service. Another problem they foresee is the age-old dilemma of rich versus poor. Properly equipped vehicles are expected to top the $55,000 price point, putting them out of the reach of mainstream car buyers.

**Ann Arbor, Michigan, and New York City** are currently serving as test cities so researchers can experiment more with autonomous and semi-autonomous driving.

In Ann Arbor, 3,000 drivers had their vehicles connected with wireless internet so they could participate in a study run by the University of Michigan, and funded by the Department of Transportation. As part of the study, sensors were installed around the city that allowed cars to connect with the existing infrastructure and other connected vehicles. Researchers are

---

[57] *What's Driving the connected car?* McKinsey & Company. September 2014.

hoping to learn how to provide a safer, smoother driving experience. To do this, the vehicles involved in the study can communicate with each other and receive information from sensors along their route. The car's onboard computer system can talk with traffic signals. When needed, it can change a stop sign to green to ensure a smoother driving experience.

The New York City test is a pilot project to help facilitate *Connected Cars*. By 2017, they hope to have 10,000 cars, taxis, trucks, and buses fitted with sensors that will allow autonomous vehicle-to-vehicle communications. The expectation is vehicle-to-vehicle communication will make for fewer accidents and smoother travel conditions. Key intersections are expected to have sensors installed that will transmit travel alerts to oncoming vehicles. The project is also developing an APP to help ensure the safety of pedestrians.

**The way I see it, the *Connected Car*** is coming, but the way it's coming together is a hot mess. Companies are working furiously to grab a lead, and secure their place in the market. But, like the *Connected House*, everyone is going their own way. It's Apple versus Google, GM versus Ford, etc., etc.

Right now, it's anybody's guess who's going to come out on top in the race to deliver the world's first fully *Connected Car* or the world's first autonomous self-driving car.

I'm going to cover these topics in the following sections.

- Infotainment systems
- On-board hot-spotting and *Connected Car* simulators
- Autonomous and semi-autonomous cars
- Ford Pass

# Infotainment Systems

**Apple and Google are currently** engaged in a furious battle to determine who will control your car's infotainment system. As with your smartphone, the decision is going to come down to IOS or Android. Pretty much all automakers offer you one system or the other. Some manufacturers give you a choice. Toyota is the only major automaker to hold out and require car buyers to go with their proprietary infotainment system.

Your smartphone is the heart of the new infotainment systems. Just connect your device via a micro USB cable, and the magic starts to happen.

The truth is both systems are very similar as far as functionality and operations go. Google's infotainment system is called Android Auto; Apple's is called Apple CarPlay.

**Apple CarPlay**

Apple aficionados probably won't be surprised when I tell them the CarPlay screen looks a lot like your iPhone display. There's a reason for that. It makes for a smooth, seamless transition from one device to the other. CarPlay users immediately see the familiar APPs they use day in and day out on their iPhones. There's nothing new to learn. That's intentional, to prevent any additional driver distraction.

The system is compatible with all iPhones starting with the iPhone 5 and above. Just connect your device to CarPlay with your micro USB plug.

The buttons on CarPlay's center counsel are big and bold. That makes them easy to find and operate while driving. Most APPs have been trimmed down so that they only go one or two levels deep. That's another safety feature Apple devised to make using CarPlay less distracting for drivers.

Drivers have several easy ways to control their system. They can use voice controls, buttons, or knobs. The choice is entirely yours, although the hope is you will stay safe and use voice commands as much as possible.

The navigation system is powered by Apple Maps and provides large clear pictures to get you on your way. Just tell Siri where you want to go, and your navigation system will respond with turn-by-turn directions. Car Play provides traffic conditions and estimated travel times. The display is big and bold, showing the names of cross streets. The left side of the screen shows printed turn-by-turn directions, to supplement Siri's voice commands. At the bottom of the screen, CarPlay displays your ETA, travel time, and miles to go. Nothing gets left to the imagination.

Need to make a phone call? Just tell Siri what you want. She will help you place a call, return a missed call, or listen to a voice mail. The phone display on your center console is intuitive and easy to use. It displays the caller's name in large print. Under that, it displays four bubbles to control the call. You can tap the red circle to end the call, mute to silence it, keypad to pull up your keypad and add a call to initiate a new call.

Text messaging is as easy as making a phone call. Siri can read or reply to your messages, so there's no need ever to look at your phone. To send a message you can use Siri's dictation feature and just speak your message. And, if someone sends you an audio message you can listen to it in their voice. One disadvantage of CarPlay versus Android Auto is CarPlay only lets you use regular SMS messaging and iMessaging. It does not support any third-party texting APPs like WhatsApp.

And, of course, you can listen to all your favorite music that you have stored on your iPhone. CarPlay gives you access to your playlists and songs. You can also listen to your vehicle's AM/FM, or satellite radio.

CarPlay users have access to a growing APPs library. Just understand, not all APPs are available for use in your car. Apple limits APPs to ones they've optimized for car use (which means APPs they've made driver friendly, with larger easier to see and use controls).

Overall CarPlay is a great, easy to use infotainment system. It's light years ahead of manufacturer systems. Most of the drawbacks are the same as those users of Android Auto will experience. The biggest issue is compatibility. There's still an "us," or "them" mentality involved. If you have an iPhone, you need to purchase a car that's compatible with Apple CarPlay. If you have an Android phone, the car you purchase needs to have an Android Auto infotainment system. With either system, you are locked into Google Maps or Apple Maps. Neither system allows access to third party navigation systems such as Tom-Tom. The only other thing users need to be aware of, and this isn't a disadvantage, so much as a safety feature. When your phone is connected to the infotainment system, the handset is disabled and will not work. This was a deliberate choice to help prevent distracted driving.

**Android Auto**

Google says Android Auto is compatible with all Android phones that run on Android Lollipop, but if you check the internet, there are reports of users who have experienced connectivity issues with a variety of phones. I've seen horror stories on the internet about users who have had trouble connecting the Samsung Galaxy S5, Samsung Galaxy S6, and LG 3, among others. The good thing is Google fixes most issues as soon as they become aware of them. So, if your phone does have a problem connecting to Android Auto, be sure to check back frequently for updates.

At its most basic level, Android Auto extends your smartphone into your car. As soon as you connect it via the micro USB cable, it moves your phone's content to your car's touch screen. As an additional bonus, your smartphone charges while it's connected to the infotainment system.

Google Maps powers the Navigation system for Android Auto. The maps are big and beautiful. It speaks turn-by-turn directions and suggests alternate routes in the event it detects bad weather or construction delays. If it determines your destination is a business, the navigation system will alert you if the business will be closed by the time you arrive. The turn-by-turn directions show up to the left of the map displayed on a large card. The top of the card displays an arrow that shows which way to turn. Below that it shows your ETA, miles left to drive, and the current time. Another benefit to using Google Maps is you will no longer need to pay for expensive updates for your navigation system. Updates occur automatically whenever your phone updates.

Starting out, Android Auto allows you to use a limited number of APPs. Google intends to vet each APP individually to ensure they are safe for use while driving. The ones they allow will all have large control buttons to make them easy to use while minimizing distraction to drivers. Like CarPlay most APPs will only be one or two layers deep. Again, that was done intentionally to limit driver distraction.

Google Now card notifications will be limited in your car. It will still display notifications on your center console, but most of them will be specific to use in your car—weather alerts, road closings, travel times, and suggestions about places to make a pit stop for food or bathroom breaks. It will also display notifications for any incoming text messages you receive.

Making and receiving calls is easy with Android Auto. Most of the time you can initiate calls with a simple voice command, although the system does provide a dial pad for those people who insist on using it. The display shows you who is calling and has a red circle under their name and picture so you can disconnect easily. To dial a call, just say the person's name or number. If you prefer, you can pull up your contact list on the center display. My feeling is Apple has a more intuitive and easy to use display panel. It has larger buttons and offers fewer choices. Because of this, there is less of a chance to distract drivers.

The default music service is Google Play Music. It will play any music you have stored locally on your device. You can't browse through your music or playlists, but you can get to any song using voice commands. Again, it's all about driver safety and minimizing distractions. You can also listen to music on Spotify, TuneIn Radio, iHeart Radio, and other APPs.

Overall Android Auto is a good solid system that will allow you to safely enjoy all the great features of your smartphone on your car's infotainment system. Ultimately, the choice of which system you purchase—Android Auto, or CarPlay—comes down to whether you own an Android or iPhone.

**If you don't have a newer car** equipped with Android Auto or Apple CarPlay, you can buy conversion units on the secondary market to replace your current radio and upgrade it to one of the two systems. Most of these systems work well and give you the same experience as having a factory-installed infotainment system.

# Connected Car Simulators

**Don't have a connected car, don't sweat it.** Several companies offer a fix for that. Among these are the Verizon hum, AT&Ts ZTE Mobley, and the Audiovox Car Connection 2.

Verizon *hum* turns your 1996 or newer vehicle into a *Connected Car*. It's a two-piece device that works like OnStar services in GM vehicles. The smaller OBD device plugs into your onboard diagnostic port. The speaker portion clips onto your visor and lets you access roadside assistance with the push of a button. There's also a *hum* APP for your smartphone that works on either IOS or Android devices.

Hum performs system diagnostics to help you discover problems early before they escalate into major mechanical breakdowns. It sends maintenance reminders so that you don't forget to change the oil, rotate the tires, or change your air filter. And, it gives you access to a mechanic's hotline. If you ever have a problem with a suggested repair or how much it should cost, you can call a certified mechanic to get his take on the situation.

If your problem is more serious, Hum can guide emergency services to you by using its GPS tracking services. They can send roadside assistance to get your car on the road again, and in the event your car gets stolen—they can help find it with the onboard

GPS services. Hum can also send your car's location to law enforcement authorities.

AT&Ts Mobley attacks a different problem. It converts your vehicle into a mobile hotspot that lets you connect up to five devices. It works in most vehicles 1996 and newer. Installation is as simple as it gets—just plug it into your OBD-II port and get ready to stream the internet in your car. The only catch is you need AT&T wireless services to make it work.

Audiovox Car Connection 2 is another option available from AT&T. Unlike Verizon hum, it doesn't turn your car into a connected car, but it does offer some unique features you can't get elsewhere.

Like Mobley and hum, it works with most vehicles 1996 and newer. Just plug it into your OBD-II port, and you are ready to go.

I wouldn't recommend it for engine diagnostics. I see its value more in keeping teenage drivers safe while they're on the road. When you combine it with the Car Connection 2 APP, you can restrict smartphone use while the vehicle is running. That means you don't have to worry about your teen texting or talking while driving. If you're forgetful, like me, it has a Lot Spot feature that gives walking directions back to where you parked your car. (Take that Mall of America!)

Which device is right for you?

If you want a *Connected Car*, with all the bells and whistles—Verizon hum would be your best choice. If you're worried about teen drivers, the Audiovox Car Connection 2 can help you track where they are, and assure you they're not texting and talking while driving. If you're on the road a lot and want to turn your car into a mobile hotspot to power everyone's devices, Mobley is the winner—hands down.

# Autonomous and Semiautonomous Driving

**Ever since we've had cars,** the dream has been to kick back and enjoy the ride while your car does all the work. This is what we call a fully autonomous or self-driving car. Right now, several manufacturers including Google, Apple, and Tesla are locked in a race to see who can bring their car to market the soonest.

Other manufacturers are developing semi-autonomous cars, or cars that can independently perform one or more driving function under the supervision of a driver. It's not as glamorous as a self-driving car, but how can you knock a car that can steer itself, or park itself with the tap of a button on your smartphone APP. That's still pretty cool.

*Gear Patrol*[58] says there are four stages of autonomous driving. They rank the level where the driver is in full control as level zero. In levels one through three, the driver still controls the vehicle. It's just a matter of how many functions the car can perform autonomously. By the time you reach level three, the car can drive itself in certain circumstances, but the driver is still responsible for what happens and can take back control of the wheel at any given time. Level four is a fully autonomous vehicle, where no driver participation is required.

---

[58] Connor, Andrew. *Semi-Autonomous Cars Bring the Self-Driving Car Closer to Reality.* Gear Patrol. October 23, 2015.

Right now, it is illegal to sell fully autonomous cars in the United States. The only self-driving cars allowed on the road today are those vehicles licensed for testing.

**Semi-Autonomous Cars**

**Semi-autonomous cars have been** with us for a while. In 2007, Lexus was the first manufacturer to offer automated parking. Since then Ford, Mercedes-Benz, and several other manufacturers have jumped on the bandwagon. When the system works, it's amazing. But, as Ford cautions with their system, you need to keep your hands on the wheel at all times—just in case. Some of the things that can cause problems are if a pedestrian or another object gets in the way and throws off your car's sensors.

Mercedes-Benz announced a new Parking Pilot System for its 2017 E-Class vehicles in Europe (it's not certain yet if U.S. cars will have the feature). Drivers can park their car remotely using a smartphone APP. The car can even fold in its side mirrors if it is parking in a tight space. To perform its magic, the car uses a series of onboard sensors and cameras to monitor how close other objects are to it.

Mercedes-Benz has also announced a new Drive Pilot technology for its 2017 E-class vehicles. Cars equipped with

Distronic Cruise Control will be able to take over steering, braking, and accelerating at speeds up to 130 mph. The vehicles do this by using onboard cameras, sensors, and the vehicle's GPS system. Mercedes says the car can even recognize posted speed limits and follow them.

Volvo offers semi-autonomous driving on their XC90 SUV. It can accelerate, brake, and steer at speeds under 50 km/h. It has a series of onboard cameras and sensors that can detect other cars, animals, and pedestrians in its path. It is programmed to keep you at a preset distance from the car in front of you.

Tesla has an Auto Pilot System in their new vehicles. The system is designed for highway use, not for stop and go driving. It can take control in certain circumstances. The vehicle can accelerate, brake, and steer itself. Once the vehicle is in motion, it can keep up with traffic and change lanes on its own. While the vehicle can drive on its own, Tesla advises drivers to keep their eyes on the road and their hands on the wheel.

*Gizmag*[59] recently reported on a recent study being conducted by MIT researchers. They're investigating a system that can take control of the steering wheel if it detects an imminent collision or an obstacle in the vehicle's path. When it detects a hazard, it will

---

[59] Ridden, Paul. *Semiautonomous driving system takes over when drivers make mistakes.* Gizmag. July 16, 2012.

steer the car back on a safe path, then turn control back over to the driver.

Like other semi-autonomous driving prototypes, it works through a series of onboard sensors, a front-facing camera, and a laser rangefinder. The system determines a safe driving distance between cars, and if the vehicle moves outside of that range, it assumes control.

Right now, semi-autonomous driving is limited, mainly to self-parking your vehicle. The newest systems coming out on Mercedes-Benz and other models in 2017 are being released in Europe, not in the U.S. So, the best I can say is true semi-autonomous driving is still a few years in the future for most of us.

**Fully Autonomous Cars**

Google is the Big Dog in self-driving cars.

They've been kicking around their self-driving car project since 2009, and have experimented with several different vehicles before landing on their proprietary bubble shaped car. Google thinks the weird shape is part of the car's charm and helps to disarm nearby drivers.

The car looks as strange inside, as it does outside. Three of the components normally found in every car are completely missing in Google's prototype vehicle. There's no steering wheel, brake pedal, or accelerator pedal. Google thinks adding them would tempt drunk drivers to hop behind the wheel, thus defeating the whole purpose of the self-driving car. They're currently asking the National Highway Traffic Safety Commission to exempt them from the requirement to include those objects. Google contends the numbers speak for themselves. Last year 33,000 people died in automobile accidents. Human error caused 94 percent of those accidents. If they can take humans out of the equation, Google thinks, it follows travel will be much safer.

In the nine years since they started the project, Google has logged over one million miles. Even though it's a self-driving car, they have a safety driver in the car whenever it goes out—just in case.

When asked about the car's weird shape, Google says it's the perfect design. The cute round bubble shape disarms other drivers. The round shape also maximizes the sensor's field of view, helping the vehicle to get a better sense of its surroundings. The black bubble on top houses many of the sensors needed to control the car. It contains lasers, radar, and cameras that allow it to detect objects from all directions. There is an onboard computer system inside the car to help it process all the data it receives.

What many people don't know has Google added an aggression level to the car's software. It ranges from mild to super-aggressive. For most of their tests, Google prefers the meek and mild button. Just remember, if they need to, they can go all Google on you. Keep that in mind, before you challenge the bubble car to a race. It can turn on you.

When you visit Google's self-driving car website, one of the things they talk about is that self-driving cars face many of the same challenges humans do. What should they do at a yellow light? Stop, or floor it, and race through? They wonder what pedestrians and stray pets are going to do. Should they wait for them to cross the street, or should they assume they will cross with the light? Heavy rain and snow are problems that can challenge self-driving cars. Currently, Google's prototype can't go on the road during bad weather. The same goes for highway construction zones. The car hasn't figured out the intricacies of traveling through them yet.

Google says self-driven cars need to answer four key questions before they can hit the road without human assistance.

1. Where am I? The car uses map and sensor information to determine what street and lane it is in.
2. What's around me? The car needs to use its sensors to determine what objects are around it, and what size they are.

3. What will happen next? It's the key question. Based on the information Google has learned from its one million miles of experimental driving, the car needs to put everything in context and determine what may happen.
4. What should I do next? Based on input from its sensors and what it has learned from previous interactions, the car needs to decide what it should do. Step on the brake? Speed up? Swerve?

Just like a human driver, the self-driving car needs to put things into context, and think on its feet.

Here's another little-known fact. Google reimaged the world to make their self-driving car project happen. They've done everything they can to stack the deck in their favor. Before Google puts a car on the street in a new locality, they send in a specialized team to map the area. And, I'm not talking about low-level maps like they use on Google maps. Before Google started testing their self-driving car in Mountain View, California, they sent in special teams to map every road the cars would travel. They recorded ultra-precise detailed maps, down to the height of every curb, and how high traffic signals are off the road.

Once the car analyzes all the map data, it uses its GPS system to determine where it is on the virtual maps. That's how it stays on course and keeps track of all the objects around it.

Currently, the self-driving car is not ready to go solo. Google is betting it can remove the kinks and hit the market by 2020.

**Apple is somewhat of a "wildcard"** in the autonomous car market. Rumors have floated around for the last several years that the tech giant was going to challenge Google in its effort to bring the first self-driving car to the market. Word on the street has it they intend to hit the market a full year before Google plans to market their self-driving car.

Many questions remain unanswered about Apple's intentions. An article in *The Atlantic*[60] speculates Apple may be looking at releasing an electric car, or a semi-autonomous vehicle first, as a method to establish itself in the automotive market, before they invest the big bucks required to develop a fully autonomous car.

*Wired Magazine*[61] thinks the Apple car may never come to market. They say Apple is just "dabbling," trying to determine what would happen if they release a car.

With Apple's penchant for secrecy, we may still be years away from knowing what they intend to do.

---

[60] Lafrance, Adrienne. *Why Would Apple Make an Electronic Car, Not a Driverless One?* The Atlantic. September 22, 2015.
[61] Bonnington, Christina. *The Curious Case of Apple's Supposed Self-Driving Car.* Wired Magazine. February 6, 2015.

# Ford Pass

**One often repeated prediction is** in the future we will no longer own cars. Instead of owning a car, ride sharing will become the new norm.

Ford recently released a new smartphone APP called FordPass that is bringing us one step closer to that vision of the future. *Mashable*[62] called it the "beginning of the end of car ownership."

*FordPass* is Ford's vision of where the automotive market is going. Ford[63] says its part of their "transformation into an auto and mobility company, (and) aims to do for car owners what iTunes did for music fans."

The APP has a virtual wallet, the same as Apple Pay that allows users to store payment methods, and to pay for mobility purchases. Starting out, they partnered with McDonald's and 7-ELEVEN. The list of participating merchants is expected to grow quickly.

Another service provided by the APP is *Ford Guides*. What the *Guides* feature does is allow people to talk with personal mobility assistants any time of the day or night. These *Guides* will be able

---

[62] Jaynes, Nick. *Ford's FordPass app is the beginning of the end of car ownership.* Mashable. January 10, 2016.
[63] *Ford Investing in Making Customer Experience as Strong as Its Cars, SUVS, Trucks and Electrified Vehicles with FordPass.* The Ford Motor Company Media Center. January 11, 2016.

to assist users with transportation (getting around from one place to another), lining up parking spaces, designing a new car, and any other mobility issues they may require assistance with.

If users own a Ford vehicle equipped with SYNC®Connect, FordPass will give them access to all the connected components of their vehicle. That means they can check the tire pressure, engage the remote start, lock and unlock doors, check the battery charge, fuel level, and much more. (General Motors users can do the same thing with the OnStar APP.)

Ford teamed up with *ParkWhiz* and *Parkopedia* to offer discounted parking services. Another Ford partner, *FlightCar*, offers free airport parking with a twist. They rent your car out when you leave it with them and share the proceeds with you. It's an Uber-like service without the driver. If the service catches on it could spell the end of personal car ownership. Anyone in need of a car for an hour, a day, a week, or any other time-period, could contact *FlightCar* to secure just the right vehicle, no matter where they are located. Look at it this way. Millennials love APPs. Unlike the generations before them, they're not hung up on car ownership. If the service catches on, Ford could easily expand that line of business and provide cars on a ride share basis, something that would totally disrupt the metrics of the American automobile market.

Does *Ford Pass* mean the end of car ownership? Ford appears to be saying this is one possible future. If that's the way things play out, they intend to be at the forefront of ride sharing.

It's a huge bet on the future, but one that could pay off large for Ford.

# Meet the Experts

- **Darius Allen** is president of CRBT. He can be reached at siamsmartphone.com.
- **Calon Alpar** is a Digital Marketer with *Better Mobile Security*.
- **John "JAQ" Andrews** is an information manager with Zco Corporation. He can be reached at http://www.zco.com/.
- **Anne Artmeier Balduzzi** is the founder of *SameGrain*.
- **Anne Louise Bannon** is a writer and columnist. Her website is www.annelouisebannon.com.
- **Mitchell Barker** is the founder of Whichvoip. He can be reached at Whichvoip.co.ca.
- **Bruce Burnet** is employed at *Healthcare Products, LLC. Alzheimer's Store*, www.alzstore.com.
- **SYL Chao** is the creator of the *Turing* phone.
- **John Dinsmore** is an Assistant Professor of Marketing at Wright State University.
- **Dennis Duty** is associated with Stayblcam, a company that makes stabilizers and accessories for cellphone cameras. You can check him out at www.stayblcam.com.

- **Lauren Fellure** is a Growth Partner at *SnapMobile* and has over five years of experience creating APPs. To find out more visit snapmobile.io.
- **George Gracin III** is a sales and marketing associate at *neoRhino IT Solutions* in Houston, Texas.
- **Kelly Graver** is a Design Lead at Snap Mobile. To find out more visit snapmobile.io.
- **Gray Hancock** is a project manager who facilitates the entire process of dark fiber deployment.
- **Wren Handman** is with Hammer and Tusk.
- **Dave Johnson** is editor-in-chief of *Techwalla*, a technology product review site. https://techwalla.com/.
- **Nolan Kier** is a Project Manager at *MESS APPs Inc*. He can be reached at www.messAPPs.com.
- **Maria Korolov** is a technology journalist. She is editor of Hypergrid Business, where she covers enterprise uses of virtual reality and reviews virtual reality hardware. She is also founder and president of Women in Virtual Reality.
- **Ben Lee** is CEO of NeonRoots. To find out more visit https://www.neonroots.com/.
- **Jack Lombard** is the founder/CEO of Chicago Website Design SEO Company. He can be reached at www.GoMedia.com.
- **Steve Manzuik** is Director of Security Research at Duo Security. He can be reached at www.duo.com.
- **C. J. McElveen** is a Digital Marketing and Content Specialist with *Fonez*. He can be reached at www.fonez.ie.

- **Mike McRitchie** is a wireless infrastructure development professional at *CriticalPath* Action. You can check out his blog at http://www.mikemcritchie.com.
- **Walter O'Brien** founder and CEO of Scorpion Computer Services, Inc., and executive producer of *Scorpion*, the hit cyber TV series on CBS.
- **Christopher Sharp** is the author of *The Last Ticket*.
- **Robert Siciliano,** author of *99 Things You Wish You Knew Before Your Identity Was Stolen*.

  http://robertsiciliano.com/

- **Austin Smith** is a Content Strategist for Neon Roots. He can be reached at www.neonroots.com.
- **Ken Smith** is Associate Principal Analyst at *Secure State*. He can be reached at www.securestate.com.
- **Wayne Smith** is president of Vertex Innovations and has helped build out country's telecom infrastructure. He played a critical role in the switch from dial-up modems to DSL.
- **Frank B. Spano, JD** is Executive Director and founder of *The Counterterrorism Institute*. For more information, visit www.ctinstitute.org.
- **Dane Theisen** is a co-founder of R We Still On Time? He can be reached at www.rwestillontime.com.

# About the Author

**My books offer** short easy to read solutions to your e-commerce problems. Most of them can be read in under an hour. The information can be used to help you sell more products on eBay and Amazon, services on Fiverr, or eBooks on Amazon and Kindle.

Selling online isn't a mystery. It doesn't even have to be difficult.

It's all about getting started. Many people I've talked with have this crazy fear of putting things up for sale on eBay and Amazon. They think they have to do this and do that; they worry they don't know enough about what they're doing to do it right; they wonder what they should sell, and they worry about whether they can even do it or not.

That's where my books come in.

They take you hand-in-hand and walk you through getting started selling on eBay, Amazon, and Fiverr. They show you how to market your Kindle book.

My goal is to help you over the speed bumps so that you can be more successful from the get-go.

What are you waiting for?

Most of my books are available as audiobooks, so if you prefer to listen rather than read, be sure to check them out.


May 15th, 2017


Nick Vulich

Davenport, Iowa

# Bonus Excerpt

*(Here's a sample from my book **History Bytes: People, Places, and Events That Shaped American History**. Read this book, and you're going to think wow! American history is full of strange paradoxes, and that's what makes it so interesting. The truth is much of what we learn about history is a series of little white lies that over time have grown into tall tales.)*

**John Wilkes Booth**

Imagine what it would be like to wake up, flip on the morning news, and discover that Bradley Cooper or Ashton Kutcher had assassinated President Obama at the movie theater. That's what happened on the morning of April 15th, 1865. People were shocked when they learned John Wilkes Booth had killed President Lincoln.

Booth was one of the most popular actors of his day. He was young, just twenty-six years old, considered one of the most attractive men in America. He stood five feet, 8 inches tall, had a lean, athletic build, ivory skin, and curly, jet black hair. Booth had a reputation as a lady's man, and women mobbed him, on and off stage.

At the time he killed Lincoln, Booth was pulling down $25,000 a year as an actor (that's roughly $500,000 in 2015 money). And, yet—he sacrificed it all for his political beliefs.

What was going on in the mind of John Wilkes Booth? What was it that turned this mild-mannered actor into one of the most hated men of his generation?

...............

John Wilkes Booth was born into a dynasty of actors.

His father, Junius Brutus Booth, was considered one of the finest Shakespearian actors of his day. He was over-fond of drink, prone to spells of near madness, and according to one source— Junius Booth penned a letter to President Andrew Jackson in 1835, threatening to kill him unless he released two pirates.

John and his brothers, Edwin, and Junius, Jr. were stage favorites. John never won the acclaim his brother Edwin did but given time; many critics feel he could have outperformed him.

Booth made his acting debut in 1855, at the age of seventeen, as the Earl of Richmond in Shakespeare's *Richard III*. He was good, but not great. There's some evidence that he often forgot his lines or missed cues, but the girl's liked him anyway—his looks compared favorably to a young Sinatra or Elvis.

He joined the Know Nothing Party (a white supremacist group that wanted to limit foreign immigrants) in the 1850s. In 1859 he enlisted in the Richmond Grays, a Virginia Militia unit that helped put down John Brown's abolitionist uprising at Harper's Ferry. After Brown's capture, Booth stood guard by the scaffold as Brown was hanged.

Booth's acting career exploded in 1860 after he engaged Matthew Canning, a Philadelphia lawyer, as his agent. He opened his professional career playing Richard III in Montgomery, Alabama. George Alfred Townsend wrote, "His conception of Richard was vivid and original, one of the best we have had."

He soon appeared in venues all over the country including—New York, Chicago, Baltimore, Boston, Washington, St. Louis, and Richmond. He was best known as a Shakespearian actor starring in Romeo & Juliet, Hamlet, Macbeth, and the Merchant of Venice. Booth made his New York Stage debut in 1862. The *New York Herald* reported he was a "veritable sensation." The Washington Intelligencer said his Romeo was "the most satisfactory of all renderings of that fine character." Abraham Lincoln was in the audience at Ford's Theater on November 9, 1863, when Booth played Raphael in *The Marble Heart*.

................

There's no doubt. Booth was a successful actor, a handsome young man, and a Southern sympathizer. The question is: What was the trigger that made him jump from Southern sympathizer to presidential assassin? Why didn't he just join the Confederate army?

Part of it was an outgrowth of his political beliefs. The Know Nothing Party was a White Supremacist group that wanted to limit immigration, especially the Catholics and the Irish. It's well-known that Booth supported slavery, and was against freeing blacks. In a letter, he wrote to his brother-in-law in November of 1864, Booth said, "This country was formed for the white, not the black man."

Booth was arrested in St. Louis in 1862 for making anti-Union remarks. It was no secret he despised Lincoln and blamed him for the South's problems. In 1864 Booth began recruiting agents to help him carry out a plot he devised to kidnap Abraham Lincoln. The original plan was to kidnap Lincoln on one of his frequent rides to the Soldier's Home outside of Washington. Once they captured him, the conspirators were going to transport Lincoln to Richmond, where the South could ransom him to end the war on their terms, or to facilitate the exchange of captured Confederate soldiers.

There is some evidence to suggest Booth was working with the Confederate government to kidnap Lincoln, but no substantial proof exists. In 1864 he met with Confederate sympathizers at Parker House in Boston, and again in October of 1864, he stayed at St. Lawrence Hall in Montreal, Canada, a known meeting place for the Confederate Secret Service.

In November of 1864, the conspirators began meeting at Mary Surratt's boarding house in Washington. Members of the group included—David Herold, George Atzerodt, John Surratt, and Lewis Payne.

On March 17th, 1865, the conspirators learned Lincoln would be attending the play, *Still Waters Run Deep*, near the Soldier's Home. Unfortunately, for Booth, Lincoln changed his plans at the last moment and ended up attending an event at the National Hotel in Washington.

Robert E. Lee surrendered to General Ulysses S. Grant on April 9th, 1865. Two days later Booth was in the audience listening to an impromptu speech Lincoln gave at the White House. As Booth listened to Lincoln talk about giving limited Negro Suffrage, he told David Herold, "That means nigger citizenship."

If there was one decisive moment where John Wilkes Booth's plans changed and moved from kidnap to murder, this was it.

...............

The Presidential Party arrived at Ford's Theater around 8:30 PM. William Withers, Jr., the orchestra leader said, they played "Hail to the Chief" as the Lincoln's entered the theater. The crowd stood up and cheered for the President. They waved handkerchiefs and hats to salute him. As Lincoln entered the Presidential Box, he smiled down at the audience and bowed to the crowd before sitting down.

The President sat in a rocker close to the balcony. Mrs. Lincoln was in an armchair next to him. Miss Harris was at the far right, and just behind her, Major Rathbone sat on the sofa.

Witnesses Booth spotted outside of Ford's Theater just before 10:00 PM. He enjoyed a brandy at an adjoining saloon and walked slowly towards the theater. He asked John Buckingham, the doorman, for the time, and made his way towards the stairs. He passed around the dress circle, moving towards the door leading to the President's Box. William Withers, Jr. saw Booth walking on the balcony, moving towards the President's Box, but didn't think anything about it because Booth was a regular visitor to the theater.

Lincoln's bodyguard that night was John Parker, a Washington, D.C. policeman. Parker stood guard in the little passageway outside of the entrance to the Presidential Box. He abandoned his post several times during the performance; once to watch the play from the first gallery. After the intermission, he disappeared altogether with Lincoln's footman and coachman to visit a nearby tavern.

One result was the Presidential Box was left unattended.

Booth crept in through the unguarded door. After entering the passageway, he grabbed a block of wood and barred the doorway shut. Chances are Booth took a moment to steady himself as he peered into the President's Box.

At 10:20 PM Booth crept through the door with his Derringer raised and leveled. He fired a ball into the back of President Lincoln's head. Lincoln slumped forward, motionless.

Inside the box, it was clouded with white smoke from the powder and shot. Mary Lincoln let out a screech. Major Henry A. Rathbone jumped to his feet and began struggling with Booth. Booth lashed out with his dagger. He thrust at Rathbone's heart. Rathbone blocked the blow with his arm. The dagger dug several inches deep into his arm and tore into his chest.

Booth broke free. Rathbone grasped at Booth's coat but didn't have the strength to hold him. Booth jumped to the stage, catching his leg in the draped flags as he leaped.

Wither's testimony gives a vivid account of what followed.

I "heard the crack of a revolver," as I returned to the orchestra. "I saw a man jump from the President's Box onto the stage. He ran directly to the door leading to the backstage. This course brought him right in my pathway. He had a dagger in his hand,

and he waved it threateningly. He slashed at me, and the knife cut through my coat, vest, and underclothing. He struck again, the point of the weapon penetrating the back of my neck, and the blow brought me to the floor. I recognized him as J. Wilkes Booth, and watched him make his exit to the alley."

Another witness to the scene, a Miss Porterfield, was attending the play with her mother. She told her story in a 1913 issue of *Century Magazine*. "We heard the report of a pistol shot, followed almost immediately by Booth's dramatic leap from the President's Box. I remember distinctly the gleam of his dagger as he descended to the stage. I heard him shout something … I could not clearly distinguish his words, of course later they were [known] "sic semper tyrannis!" "The South is avenged!"

"Looking up to the box, "I could not see the President, but I could see Mrs. Lincoln and hear her shrieks and moans."

In confusion, most people thought it was all part of the play – the shot (if they heard it at all) and Booth's dramatic leap to the stage.

Booth rushed into the alley, grabbed the reigns to his horse from John Burroughs, knocked him to the ground, and headed out at full gallop through the streets of the Capitol.

Major Rathbone picked himself up and unbarred the door. Miss Harris screeched, "The President is shot."

By this time several doctors arrived and began assessing the President's condition. They laid him on the floor and began stripping off his clothes. Moments later they discovered a bullet in his head. The ball entered the back of his head behind the left ear and embedded itself in his brain.

Once the doctors discovered the source of the wound, they determined to remove Lincoln to the nearest bed and do whatever they could to comfort him. Volunteers carried Lincoln out of the theater. A man across the street invited them to use his room, so they carried the President in, and laid him on a bed. Surgeon Charles Taft said it was a gruesome scene. As they carried Lincoln, "blood [was] dripping from the wound, faster and faster."

Inside Petersen House, friends and family held a vigil over the dying Lincoln. Surgeon Charles Taft spent most of the night holding the President's head, so blood and brain tissue could continue to ooze out, and prevent clotting. He was relieved several times by surgeon Charles H. Crane.

Lincoln passed away at 7:22 the next morning, April 15th, 1865.

They wrapped his body in a flag taken from the Tenth Street House. The President's remains were placed in a cart and paraded through the streets of Washington to the White House.

..............

Lincoln wasn't the only target that night.

Lewis Thornton Powell rang the bell at William Seward's Mansion about 10:00 PM. He told the doorkeeper he was delivering medicine for Seward. Powell made his way upstairs to Seward's bedroom.

Frederick Seward, the son of Secretary Seward, confronted Powell at the top of the stairs. Powell started down the stairs, turned, and attacked Frederick Seward with the butt of his revolver. When he heard the commotion Seward's nurse assistant, Sergeant George E. Robinson, rushed out to help. Powell struck him in the forehead with his knife and raced to Secretary Seward's bed, where he stabbed him three times in the neck.

As Powell was getting ready to strike Seward again, Sergeant Robinson and Major August H. Seward pulled him away. Powell broke free, and made his escape, stabbing a messenger as he ran out of the house.

Alone, and without assistance, Powell hid out in a nearby cemetery for three days. Not knowing where to meet up with his fellow-conspirators, he returned to the one place he knew they frequented — Mary Surratt's Washington boarding house. His timing couldn't have been worse. When he arrived there, authorities were searching the boarding house. Both Lewis Powell and Mary Surratt were taken into custody.

George A. Atzerodt had a room at Kirkwood House, just below Vice-President Andrew Johnson's. His job was to kill the Vice-President. Instead, he got drunk and wandered the streets of Washington. He was later discovered hiding in the home of a relative.

Michael O'Laughlen boarded General Ulysses S. Grant's train to Philadelphia on the afternoon of April 14th, 1865. His mission was to kill Grant, but he couldn't gain access to Grant's private car because it was locked and guarded by porters.

www.ingramcontent.com/pod-product-compliance
Lightning Source LLC
Chambersburg PA
CBHW021405170526
45164CB00002B/514